S Martin's College, Lancaster
1964–89

by
Peter S. Gedge
and
Lois M. R. Louden

Centre for North-West Regional Studies
University of Lancaster

1993

General Editor, Oliver M. Westall

A History of S Martin's College, Lancaster 1964-89
by
Peter S. Gedge and Lois M. R. Louden

This volume is the twenty-eighth in a series published by the Centre for North-West Regional Studies at the University of Lancaster. Details of other titles in the series which are available may be found at the back of this volume.

ISSN 0308–4310

First edition, 1993

Published by the Centre for North-West Regional Studies, University of Lancaster
Designed and typeset by Carnegie Publishing Ltd., 18 Maynard Street, Preston
Printed and bound in the UK by H. Charlesworth & Co., Huddersfield

British Library Cataloguing-in-Publication Data
A CIP catalogue record for this book is available from the British Library

ISBN 0-901800-27-9

378
42
LIV

Contents

The College site.

Introduction

Lancaster is proud of its contribution to higher education. Two significant institutions opened there in the early 1960s—the University and S Martin's College.

S Martin's illustrates well the great changes which affected teacher training after the Robbins Report. It began in 1964 as 'Lancaster Training College', founded by the Church of England as its last contribution to the system of teacher training colleges.

This book shows how one college coped with changing government policies for higher education which devastated the training college sector. Rather surprisingly it emerged twenty-five years later to celebrate its Silver Jubilee as 'S Martin's College of Higher Education'. Retaining some sense of being a Christian community, it 'diversified' from teacher education into offering degrees in liberal arts, youth work and nursing as well, and it made important contributions to the life of the North West.

The authors had long experience within the College. Peter Gedge, who was teaching in Lancaster when it opened, was appointed to the staff in 1968 and held a succession of senior posts from 1970. Lois Louden joined the Education Department in 1975, being promoted Principal Lecturer in 1986.

This paper is dedicated to the two Principals, Hugh Pollard and Robert Clayton, whose leadership spanned the twenty-five years, and to all, staff and students, who contributed to the life and work of S Martin's College, Lancaster.

Thanks are due to the Governing Body of the College who gave a grant towards the costs of publication.

Lancaster College of Education is conceived

The Church of England first became involved in the training of teachers early in the nineteenth century when dioceses began setting up small 'model' schools to train monitors. The type of teacher training college which remained dominant for over a century began with what was undoubtedly one of the most important educational establishments to be founded in England in the first half of the nineteenth century. Government grants towards the erection of normal or model schools had first become available in 1839. Small Anglican colleges were then founded, some of which celebrated 150 years of work in 1989. In 1840 Dr J. P. Kay, later Sir James Kay-Shuttleworth, founded St John's, an Anglican residential men's college at Battersea. For good or ill, it established the residential college as the standard pattern for teacher training.

The control of teacher training by the Church of England and other voluntary bodies (including the Methodist and Roman Catholic churches) remained unbroken until the foundation of education departments in the new civic universities in the 1890s. Then the 1902 Education Act gave statutory bodies powers to build colleges. It was only when a 75 per cent building grant was offered that Local Education Authorities acted and by 1914 twenty LEA colleges had been founded. Thus the virtual monopoly of the training college field by voluntary denominational bodies was broken. Yet even in 1942 only 29 training colleges, containing half the students in training, were controlled by LEAs while there were 25 Church (of England) colleges

besides a number of colleges sponsored by other bodies in England and Wales. However, these were typically enclosed, single-sex and small, varying from 90 to 196 students.

1944 was the start of a new era for the church colleges. The McNair Committee, which had been set up in 1942 to investigate the present sources of supply and the methods of recruitment and training of teachers, stated bluntly in its Report that the Church colleges were exceedingly ill-equipped and housed. For the first time in the twentieth century state aid of 50 per cent of the capital cost of new or improved buildings was offered to voluntary colleges without requiring any change in the regulations covering admission of students.

Three courses were open to the Church of England: it could abandon its colleges; it could concentrate its efforts; it could improve all its colleges. The bitter memories of 1932 when three colleges had had to close still remained. That some in the Church saw the need to adopt a more modern approach in the colleges was shown by the publication in 1945 of a realistic and far-sighted paper.

This already noted the growing secularism in society and identified three distinctive functions for the Church colleges: to deepen and train the religious life of those who enter as Church members; to make wise and sympathetic provision for the religious life of those of other communions; to exercise a missionary ministry to those who may have had little instruction in the Christian faith. It commented that this could be very rewarding.

So in 1946 the Church Assembly of the Church of England made a crucial policy decision. It accepted in principle the responsibility of the Church—not individual dioceses—for securing the future of the Church Training Colleges. A Development Plan was accepted in 1947 but money was short and a new effort was required.

In 1949 Canon Cockin, then Secretary to the Council of Church Training Colleges, challenged the Church. 'There are conflicting views on the nature of the Church's responsibility but the Church, as the Church of England, cannot be indifferent to the religious teaching of all the children of this country.' (Religious Instruction had been made compulsory for all pupils under the 1944 Education Act.) 'Christian teachers are needed ... Our colleges have a distinctively missionary, in addition to a pastoral, responsibility.' A progress report in 1957 claimed that the expenditure of considerable sums (£1,300,000 over a decade) had led to a 'rise in morale, a sharpening of a sense of vocation of a Church college, and an improvement in academic standards.' However it also said: 'There can be no finality to the development of training colleges'.

The truth of these words was shown all too soon. In 1958 the Minister of Education announced that the training course for teachers was to be extended from two to three years from 1960. A further 12,000 places would be needed by 1962 and this figure was soon increased to 16,000. If the Church was to contribute to this then it implied more heavy expenditure although grants for buildings were increased to 75 per cent. However this seems to have been regarded as a challenge to be met boldly so the expansion policy continued.

Building a new college was even suggested. It was claimed that the Church colleges stood for something significant, even influential, in the educational field. It was also argued that the Church had no direct stake in the vast and increasingly influential sphere of higher education except the training colleges, which under the envisaged development would come academically nearer university status. At this time the colleges were a significant distinctive sector in the higher education system when the university sector was still small.

So by 1961 to a total of 4,964 places in Church colleges a further 2,788 were being added, partly by the decision to found Christ Church College in Canterbury. But again events overtook the Church. The rising birth rate led to a call for 8,000 more places nationally. The Central Board of Finance now merely recommended that the Church should keep to its proportion of college places at over 20 per cent (a great change in only twenty years) by taking up not 1,600 of the extra places but only 1,200. However, the building of a second new college was proposed, 'probably in the north'. The Church Assembly accepted the need to expand but queried the need for a second new college. The Church was realising more clearly that its work in higher education needed to be on a wider front. For example chaplaincies were developing in many new polytechnics and universities, as at the University of Lancaster. Doubt was expressed about the possibility of building a relationship between a college and a university. However after debate an expansion to 9,020 students was projected and it was agreed to set up a new college in Lancaster, the last such institution funded by the Church of England.

A view of Lancaster from the Willie Tom.

A group of students.

2

The conversion of
Bowerham Barracks (1962–4):
Lancaster College of Education begins

1. *A Steering Committee is formed*

Why had Lancaster been chosen as the site for the second new Church training college? According to Reggie Harvey, then Secretary of the Council of Church Training Colleges, criteria were carefully considered: the new college should fill a gap, be close to a university (preferably a new one), have access to schools (including a substantial proportion of church schools), be welcomed by the local authority (prepared to make a financial contribution), and have an adequate site in or near a town. After finding no suitable site in the East Midlands, attention turned to an area in the Anglican Province of York, north of Liverpool and west of the Pennines.

Lancaster then met these criteria in a remarkable way: a church college there would fill a large gap north of Chester; a university was to be sited there; nearly half the primary schools in Lancashire were Voluntary Aided (and over half of these were Church of England); it was in the jurisdiction of Charles Claxton, Bishop of Blackburn, then Chairman of the Council of Church Training Colleges; the City was most welcoming (and donated £25,000, a substantial sum in those days) and, as the Town Clerk, Don Waddell, showed, the redundant King's Own Royal Regiment Depot at Bowerham, half a mile from the centre of Lancaster, had excellent potential as a college site.

So, in October 1962 a Steering Committee met in Lancaster Town Hall. Its membership illustrates the range of groups interested. Chairman was Bishop Charles Claxton, whose strong support and clear guidance were greatly valued by the first Principal and who saw the College firmly established before retiring in 1971. The College owed much to his leadership and infectious enthusiasm. Appropriately, Don Waddell, as Town Clerk, was invited to attend all meetings; he served on the Governing Body until the 1990s, mostly as Vice-Chairman.

2. *The College site and architect*

Bowerham Barracks was in fact a much better site than its name suggests and Dr Pollard had a vision of its potential. Situated within the city on a hill, it commanded superb views over Morecambe Bay to the Lake District mountains. The principal buildings used local stone in a sober, Victorian style and were not difficult to adapt, so that the college opened only two years later in the former Officers' Mess and 'Keep' (Armoury). This site was valued at £14,000 for the buildings and £66,000 for the 36 acres of land—but finally a price was agreed at £70,000!

Charles Pike was invited to be the architect because of his experience in college work. Final plans were soon prepared and an opening proposed in 1965—soon brought forward to a pilot entry in 1964. One feature was the breaking up of the bleak barrack square by three 3-storey halls of residence, a dining hall,

Steering Committee

The College was lucky to be supported by a good 'mix' of significant people. The central Church authority was represented by Brigadier Miller (Church of England Central Board of Finance), Dr Kathleen Bliss (Secretary of the Church of England Board of Education) and Reggie Harvey (Secretary of the Council of Church Training Colleges). Local Church leaders were Bishop Bulley (Penrith), Canon Desmond Carroll (Director of Education for the Diocese of Blackburn). Percy Lord served as Chief Education Officer for Lancashire and Professor Stephen Wiseman as Director (responsible for academic relations) of the University of Manchester Area Training Organisation. The City sent two experienced men, Councillor C. Preston and Alderman C. B. Treu. The recently retired Headmaster of Lancaster Royal Grammar School, Mr R. R. Timberlake, also joined it, retaining an active link with the College until he finally left the Governing Body at the age of ninety.

The College site

The College site was originally a barracks completed in 1880 for the King's Own Regiment. The buildings became redundant in 1959 as the army reduced in numbers. Solidly built of local stone, most were adapted by the College's architect, Sir Charles Pike, but the Guard Room was swiftly demolished. The imposing 'keep', so typical of Victorian barracks, was originally the armoury. Its rooms served variously as library, resources centre, tutorial rooms, audio-visual aids department and computer centre. Later the distinguished Bridges Library was added on one side and the Cross Building on the other.

The Officers' Mess became 'College Main', the base for college administrators - and sometimes a target for student campaigns! The anteroom and Officers' Dining Room proved ideal for the Senior Common Room, an invaluable friendly meeting place for staff. The barrack blocks were converted into lecture and tutorial rooms, and two blocks of married quarters became student residences. The Drill Hall provided one of the two gymnasia, and the quartermaster's stores became the Art Department.

The large barrack square was cleverly broken up by three other halls of residence and teaching accommodation, built of local stone and pale brick, interspersed with lawns, trees and flower beds. At the south end is a dining hall with distinctive roof; on the north side the chapel dominates the College entrance symbolically.

The 'Other Ranks' dining hall (of corrugated iron) and the low miniature rifle range were soon replaced by Student Common Rooms and the 'College Range' lecture rooms. Over all looms the 'Willy Tom', a nine-storey block of student rooms typical of its period.

Thus was created a pleasant campus for 700 students.

King's Own on Parade (King's Own Royal Regimental Museum, Lancaster)

a laboratory and a long corridor providing tutorial rooms and a lecture theatre. A 'fan-shaped' chapel to seat 400 was (as the first College prospectus states) 'deliberately placed in a central position at the main entrance to the campus, and designed not only to form the focal point of the entire layout but also to indicate the close relationship of the church and the daily life of the College'.

Work on the site began in January 1964. The Guard Room was rapidly demolished and an Assembly Hall constructed, named after Princess Margaretha of Sweden, as a symbol of the developing Swedish connection. The site also had a potential for future buildings which proved invaluable as student numbers expanded.

The choice of Charles Pike was inspired. His use of local stone and pale brick enabled the new to blend happily with the old and with careful landscaping created a campus which is admired as a pleasant place in which to live and work.

However, all this had to be paid for, so an Appeal Committee was set up to contribute to the Church's share of the cost (at that time 25 per cent) and to repay the money originally provided by the Church Assembly. This appeal made slow progress after the City's donation of £25,000, apart from two spectacular donations by East Lancashire folk. William Thompson gave £50,000, gaining as his memorial the naming of the 9-storey block as the William Thompson Hall of Residence, known irreverently by generations of students as the 'Willy Tom'. His sister soon after gave £15,000 similarly commemorated by the Sarah Witham Thompson Hall.

timer Pollard as Principal, in December 1962. He had 'the sheer force of a unique personality combined with a genuine care for individuals'. He was very conscious that the College was only the second Church of England College to be founded in the twentieth century and he had a clear vision of the sort of Christian educational community he intended to create—academically, culturally, socially and spiritually. He immediately set about achieving this 'with every fibre of his being', starting work on 1 July 1963 in an office in a remote part of the Town Hall.

3. Principal Hugh Mortimer Pollard

The quality of leadership is crucial in any enterprise and S Martin's ethos was determined by the selection, through the strong support of Bishop Claxton, of Hugh Mor-

4. Getting under way

His energy and total commitment were needed as everything had to be done even more quickly when the opening was brought forward one year.

The 'Willy Tom' and, on the right, the Keep

Dr Hugh Mortimer Pollard

Dr Pollard's experiences admirably fitted him for the post of Principal. He was a native of East Lancashire, well known in the region. He had read English at Wadham College, Oxford in the 1930s and was clearly influenced by the style of life there. After teaching in Newton Abbot, he served in the army, creating at the end of the War a school out of ruins in Berlin. He lectured at Chester, one of the oldest Church training colleges.

He had done research for a PhD on *Pioneers of Popular Education*, including James Kay-Shuttleworth who established a very significant church college in the 1840s. At Sheffield University, he came under Professor Harold Dent, who was a strong influence on the early development of S Martin's. When appointed to S Martin's, he was vice-principal of another early church college, St Mark and St John, Chelsea (a continuation of Kay-Shuttleworth's college), then enduring severe strains of expansion. He was a devoted Anglican with high academic and cultural standards.

What should the College be called? Eventually, after the Robbins Report on higher education, the title of 'Lancaster College of Education' was accepted. (There had in fact been two earlier Lancaster Training Colleges: 1920–1922 in the Storey Institute for prospective local elementary school teachers and 1946–1950 as an Emergency Teacher Training College for 200 ex-servicemen in what was then the Ripley Hospital Orphanage.) A Trust Deed was needed. A fine educational environment had to be created and resources begged for. The architect's plans and estimates had to be scrutinised and modified to fit the money available—and no Bursar was available until Ernest Helm started on 13 January 1964. Local goodwill had to be secured at all levels. Visits had to be made and contacts with potentially useful people developed. Students had to be recruited to produce a College of originally 400 three-year Certificate students, soon raised to 500. Courses had to be devised to meet the requirements of the University of Manchester in whose Area Training Organisation the college was sited. Already the possibility of teaching the new

BEd degree and adding a Post Graduate Certificate in Education was raised—which proved vital to the college's later survival. Above all suitable staff had to be appointed.

First was the Vice-Principal, Dr Gwen Owen, Headmistress of Brighouse Girls' Grammar School. She made light of administration but was in reality shrewd, efficient—and forceful! Others soon followed, to start on 1 April 1964. Bill Etherington came from St John's College, York, to be Head of Education and Dean of Men (caricatured as ensuring that men students went into school properly dressed and with hair cut short). Pollard liked to appoint 'characters' (with a penchant for Oxbridge graduates). Many were young and most served the college until they retired.

5. Fundamental Principles

From the start the principle was established that staff should have sound teaching experience (with a professional qualification) as well as being academically acceptable to the

University. Thus until the 1980s all staff not only gave academic lectures but also were involved in professional courses and in supervising teaching practice. But the predominance of grammar school teachers on the staff—typical of colleges developing in the late 1960s—meant that the professional training for primary students took some time to develop. These principles were far-sighted. Not only did they enable the College to meet future varied academic and professional demands but they also prevented the common division between 'academics' and 'professionals' and maintained a staff corporate feeling which weathered the storms of the 1970s.

To stretch students intellectually, academic standards were to be high. Staff wore gowns and students wore them on formal occasions initially. In addition to 'Curriculum subjects' (English, Mathematics, etc.) and 'the Principles and Practice of Education', students were all to take two academic 'subjects of special study'. Maintaining this academic emphasis, while developing standards of professional work, also stood the College in good stead as the teacher education colleges evolved rapidly in the next twenty years to become integral parts of the higher education system.

The religious life of the new College exercised Hugh Pollard greatly. He set out to counter the tendency, experienced so widely in the expanding Church colleges of the 1960s, to dilute any Christian ethos—even to produce a bitterly divided institution. He aimed to 'produce men and women convinced that, without a Christian basis, education lacks its only sure foundation.' The Chaplain was of central importance—and was not to be an academic lecturer to leave him free for pastoral duties. He sought a member of a religious community and the Society of the Sacred Mission provided Chaplains for ten years. The Holy Communion service was given a central place as a focus for the life of the evolving College from the start, the original members of staff starting this tradition even in the term before the students arrived.

Against the times—and in the face of hostility from some University academics—Dr Pollard resolutely set out to shortlist and appoint staff who were not only academically able but also Christians or at least sympathetic to the Christian principles of the college. He also intended to set up a tutorial system whereby a group of about ten students met a member of staff weekly for serious discussion to help them to make a decision about a philosophy of life. Christians would wish to argue that all this contributed significantly to one important feature of the College which students and visitors have commented on frequently—its caring atmosphere.

6. Preparing for the first intake of students

The Lancaster College of Education legally came into being in April 1964 with its Trust Deed and the Governing Body held its first meeting on 14 April.

21 April 1964 was the first day of term for the new College, according to the Principal's book in which—as was his custom—he wrote down everything he wanted to say at meetings. He continued as he addressed his core staff 'I hope it will be a place of refinement, civilisation and intellectual distinction ... I hope it will acquire ... an ethos of its own. But I hope most of all that it will prove to be a place with the Christian religion running through every detail of its life ...' As he reported to the governors at their second meeting in July, it was a period of 'consolidation and preparation during which a common policy was established'.

He strove hard to build a team out of these disparate characters, committed to the new enterprise of creating the latest—and what proved to be the last—Church of England College of Education to be founded and Frank Warren, the first Head of English, recalled 'a seemingly inevitable air of dedication'. He reported to them weekly, initiating his policy of keeping all his staff informed—another feature which helped staff to feel more secure. Already he was planning an unusual Academic Board to include all staff and by July two members of staff were elected on to the Governing Body. Tutors taught in local primary schools and visited others. He made them each lead a seminar on a religious book. They met all sorts of interesting folk. And every Friday, they celebrated Holy Communion together.

Around this core programme, manifold activities and planning continued hectically to be ready to start teaching 80 Certificate students in September. Warren emphasised that the relative smoothness of the College's beginning was to a very large degree due to this period of preparation. The Department of Education and Science [DES] gave permission for a PGCE to start in 1966.

Teaching for degrees and not merely the Certificate of Education had been envisaged from the start by Dr Pollard, and discussions arose over the new four-year BEd degree recommended by the Robbins report. This would be a striking advance in the academic demands hitherto expected of training colleges, which some university academics found hard to accept.

Already problems were arising over relationships with not merely one University—Manchester—but two, as the new University of Lancaster which admitted its first students in 1964 was considering how to involve itself in 'Education'. After a meeting in the DES a working party was set up to consider the possibility of College students reading for degrees there. Student questions were discussed—securing decent lodgings, Friday tutorial groups, breaking a 'five-day week mentality', maintaining high standards of dress. Then at last the College had a proper name. The converted barracks were named after a Roman soldier converted to a Christian bishop—S Martin.

First students and staff. (Lancaster Guardian)

3

An ethos is established (1964–7)

1. The first intake of students

So only two years after the Steering Committee first met, the College opened on 23 September 1964, with 89 students and 13 staff attending an Inaugural Service in the College Library in the presence of the Vice-Chancellor of the University of Lancaster, Mr Charles Carter. A more official service was held on 9 October in the former Drill Hall when Dr Coggan, the Archbishop of York, dedicated the College.

'It was not a gentle birth; at times it has been in the nature of a hurricane,' Frank Warren recalled, as 'pathetically little' of the campus was as yet available and conditions resembled living on a building site; but, the Dean said, 'It was a marvellous experience.' All agree that the Principal was the prime mover. He managed to get the first set of students very keen with a real consensus and enthusiasm. 'It was an extension of the family at home,' according to one student; non-academic staff were homely, governors made a real effort to know students and staff; the Principal 'talked to you', and 'we were generally valued as people.' Students loved the games at his Sunday night parties. Many recall his perambulations—in cap and gown—through all areas of the college (picking up any litter!). Weekly tutorial groups developed relationships between students and staff and student self-confidence. A Student Council, not yet a universal feature in colleges, was started. Social activities were put on—sports (with the Engineer, Harry Harrison, training the soccer team), a college pilgrimage to Cartmel Priory on S Martin's day (11 November), a Christmas concert and formal dinner and

Ball, singing the Schütz Passion in Christ Church, an ode on May Morning from the keep. Students proudly wore the College scarf in grey and sapphire blue (designed by the Queen's milliner), the College of Heralds authorised a crest and, after learned discussions, a Latin motto was adopted: *Scio cui credidi* (I know Him in whom I have believed). For in this year no-one thought of not attending the weekly Friday Eucharist which was Dr Pollard's attempt to focus the community consensus without resorting to the compulsory daily chapel services still to be found in some Church colleges. The Bishop of Salisbury's Commission on *The Communication of the Christian Faith* (whose brief included yet another appraisal of the value to the Church of England of its training colleges) commented to Dr Pollard that their visit was in many ways the most stimulating and encouraging of all their visits to colleges. So Dr Pollard felt able to say 'We have settled into a happy community'.

Underlying his apparent affectation and eccentricities lay a deep spiritual purpose—the growth of individuals and the institution. He wanted to expose people to the first-rate and was determined that the College should establish a good reputation quickly. Society in the 1960s still expected much of teachers so 'standards' were stressed in work, behaviour and dress and at first no-one questioned this. One result certainly was that the City rapidly accepted the College. But his horizons were wider—to extend the students. He brought in a range of visitors. He started staff 'colloquia'; he began to collect art treasures, as Church College principals did. He developed a link with Sweden which was attracting interest in

England because of the quality of its art and design and its distinctive educational system.

His academic vision was broad: 'You are not here to train as teachers but to further your Education', one student recalls him saying. This Oxbridge notion was important when so many had a low view of the academic level of 'training colleges'. It did much to secure the survival of the College in the 1970s but was distinctive at a time when some colleges training primary teachers were moving away under the influence of the Plowden report *Children and their primary schools* from a study of distinct academic disciplines. The College envisaged from the start teaching for degrees and, to stretch the students intellectually, all took two main subjects (no 'subsidiaries') besides the Theory of Education and 'Curriculum Subjects'. For two years there were even lectures on Saturday mornings! But, in fact, it soon proved too demanding for some students and was modified. This was hardly surprising when minimum entry qualifications then were five GCE 'Ordinary level' passes and the average College of Education student was rarely academically ambitious.

However, S Martin's always attached great importance to teaching practice. All staff—not merely Education lecturers—were expected to supervise it and soon the policy was established of sending students out for two periods each of virtually a term's length instead of the short periods found in many colleges. This gave students a sound appreciation of the role of a class teacher and helped

Initial Governing Body

Chairman	Bishop of Blackburn
Representatives of:	
Archbishop of York	Bishop of Lancaster
	R. M. Sibson
Diocese of Bradford	Revd E. J. G. Rogers
Diocese of Carlisle	Bishop of Penrith
Blackburn Diocesan Council for Religious Education	Canon Carroll
	R. R. Timberlake
City of Lancaster	Councillor Preston
	Alderman C B Treu
Lancashire Education Committee	Percy Lord
	Miss F. M. Openshaw
University of Lancaster	Vice Chancellor
University of Manchester	Prof S. Wiseman
	Mr. G. A Ashworth
Central Board of Finance	Brig Miller
Church Board of Education	Mr G. Sale
coopted	Stephen Jeffreys (University)
	D Waddell (Town Clerk)

A controversial 'Crucifixion'.

the College rapidly to increase its intake. Ever increasing numbers of students in areas of low population forced the College to look as far afield as the Isle of Man and Scotland for school places.

No 'training college' had academic independence and Manchester University took responsibility initially for S Martin's courses. Relationships were friendly but exacting as negotiations over the introduction of the new Bachelor of Education [BEd] degree were to show. However, the University of Lancaster also rapidly developed relationships with S Martin's, through the good offices especially of its first Vice-Chancellor, Charles Carter, who had a vision of a University for the North West with associated Colleges of Education. Both institutions were new and still small so members of staff met socially and formally. Already Charles Carter was considering the possible implications for his Univer-

sity of the Government's decision that any link between university and colleges of education should be academic but not administrative. As early as February 1965 he told the Governing Body that a 'degree of the University of Lancaster should mark the successful completion of a controlled educational process, not simply success in a final examination'. This implied that the University 'should approve the general organisation and methods of each College as well as recognising selected teachers and courses within it'. The notion was raised of Lancaster's taking over from Manchester the academic supervision of the four nearest Colleges—Poulton le Fylde, Chorley (a new non-residential training college) and the historic Charlotte Mason College in Ambleside, besides S Martin's. All this was to result in the foundation of the University of Lancaster School of Education in 1967 and to complicate the College's academic planning. But the School's Secretary, George Cockburn, rapidly developed and maintained good administrative relationships.

Another complication was the 'leitmotif' of the 1960s—the Robbins Report's call for a rapid expansion in teacher training places to meet the need for more teachers. Several factors justified this policy then: the extension of the Teacher's Certificate course from two years to three; the increased birthrate (expected to continue); a desire to reduce class sizes; raising the school leaving age to sixteen; and the growing demand for higher education before universities had expanded. (The colleges of education were still a significant separate sector in higher education, particularly for young women, a situation which changed drastically in the 1970s.) Consequently, Governing Body and Academic Board meetings wrestled with the problem of how to answer DES insistence on raising student targets.

As Dr Pollard said in his 1965 report to the Manchester School of Education, 'it was, in fact, a very hectic year ... All in all [it] was extremely exciting and rewarding, despite those ever present problems inevitably associated with the creation of a new foundation.'

2. Pressure to expand

170 students were eventually recruited in 1965 and 158 in 1966, though finding suitable men was not easy and women always formed a large majority. The Department of Education and Science [DES] aimed at a 'balance of training' and the proportions were set at 35 per cent Infant/Junior, 25 per cent Junior, 30 per cent Junior/Secondary, 10 per cent Secondary. The colleges were still seen as a source of secondary teachers though national policy from 1961 was for the universities to dominate this phase of training. (McGregor, 1991, p. 174) Fourteen new staff joined, two subjects were added—French and History—and three sciences were offered though only Biology recruited satisfactorily. Inevitably the

original spirit of consensus could not be maintained at the same level.

The pressure to expand exercised Governors and staff greatly. The DES had played its common trick of publishing a significant circular just as the long vacation started. 'College letter 7/65' demanded increased 'productivity' and suggested five schemes. The need to recruit more mature students was soon stressed as well. The College refused to be rushed as it was so new, but finally agreed to introduce a 'Box and Cox' scheme from 1967 under which one year group would be out for each term on Teaching Practice.

3. New developments—PGCE and BEd

The introduction of the Post Graduate Certificate in Education course proved extremely significant for the future of the College. Government policy was to raise the proportion of graduate teachers outside the grammar schools and the DES wanted S Martin's to start a course. As early as October 1965, the Vice-Chancellor made a momentous suggestion—that the University would found a Department of Educational Research but not start a PGCE course; its students would go to S Martin's provided that the 'problem' of its being a denominational college could be overcome and sufficiently high grade staff were present. Ten students were recruited in 1966. The number rose rapidly, peaking at 193 in 1973, the largest group in a Church College. It enriched the professional side of the college and in the savage 'cuts' of the 1970s it proved an invaluable life-line. But the comment of Bishop Bulley proved perceptive: it was more important to develop a four-year BEd course in which influence over students could grow than to place undue emphasis on a PGCE course involving students (usually non-resident) who would be in the college for only one year.

A modification of the Certificate course was worked out to start in 1967. 'Method' work continued to develop and the weight of the second academic subject was slightly reduced. Another major influence on academic planning was the introduction of the new BEd degree which marked a significant advance in the academic level of colleges of education. Seven universities introduced it in 1967—not all at honours level. Manchester planned for a 1968 start, adding a fourth year to 'top up' the Certificate. This raised questions of sufficiently advanced course content in the Certificate (at least in its third year) and suitable staff and resources. Stringent 'visitations' were made in 1966 and deficiencies in some subjects had to be remedied. Matters were complicated further by agreement that the University of Lancaster should establish its own School of Education which would be responsible from 1967 for the academic courses and examinations at S Martin's and the three other local colleges while the Manchester Area Training Organisation retained responsibility for general policy matters. Lancaster, under Professor Alec Ross as Director of the School, adopted the same model of BEd degree (ie a Certificate plus a fourth year) and was progressive enough to offer it from the start at Honours level only. Transitional arrangements were therefore necessary to enable 1965 entry students completing a Manchester Certificate in 1968 to progress to a Lancaster BEd in 1968–9.

These complex issues were discussed not only by the Governors but by the entire academic staff because the Principal had set up an Academic Board to which all staff (including the Medical Officer) belonged so that all would know what was going on and feel free to talk to him. So, the recommendations of the Weaver Report (1966), which sought to secure for the academic staff of a college the ultimate responsibility for academic direction, raised the issue for S Martin's not of securing greater involvement of staff but of reducing the size of the Board to give greater weight to the staff with greater responsibility. However the membership of the College's Board remained unchanged as it was felt important to keep younger members of staff fully informed and to give them the opportunity for greater involvement in decision making. In practice senior staff greatly influenced the running of the College through regular Heads of Subject meetings. Interestingly it was not yet felt appropriate to have student representation on either the Academic Board or the Governing Body.

Another report which provoked discussions in the Church Colleges was that on *The Communication of the Christian Faith* (1966). It pointed out the strains being imposed on the colleges as Christian communities by rapid expansion. It was profoundly impressed by their potential importance in the missionary strategy of the Church (p. 38) 'when perhaps seldom more than a quarter [of the students] would call themselves active Christians.' (p. 8) But a central issue at S Martin's— as in other Church colleges—remained that of staffing. The Academic Board agreed that staff should at least 'be able from personal commitment to support the Christian aims of the College'. Finding such staff, however, proved difficult.

4. Phase II is completed

Staff continued to grow to meet student numbers. Already the policy of improving staff qualifications began—so vital in the battle for survival in the 1970s. Primary lecturers who were not graduates were sent off to get a degree; graduates were seconded to obtain a higher degree.

The first annual Swedish lecturer came in 1965 and a Swedish connection developed. Princess Margaretha of Sweden opened the William Thompson Hall of Residence in March 1966, Sigurd Persson designed furniture for the chapel dedicated in May 1967. Einar Forseth produced a delightful stained glass window of S Martin dividing his cloak for the beggar. At last Phase II of the building programme was reaching completion and Anglican prelates blessed successive parts.

Chapel at the centre.

Princess Alexandra, Chancellor of the University, opened the Art Department informally; Dr Chippendale had a fine medical centre with a resident nurse; the scientists had their own laboratories instead of working off site (at the College of Further Education) under great difficulties; in-service work with teachers and raising money by vacation conferences had begun; all the halls of residence were completed to give 230 places. The grounds were carefully planted. From a bleak barracks had been created a college campus of high quality.

More works of art were added—splendid chapel silver by David Mellor, Barbara Hepworth's 'Winged Figure', loans from Abbot Hall, a bequest by Guy Barton, the controversial Bratby 'Crucifixion'. Musical events were put on, most notably a lieder recital by the world famous soprano Elisabeth Schwarzkopf.

And so the first intakes completed their courses. The final teaching practice results were satisfactory. In the final examinations, sixty-five obtained the Teacher's Certificate, nine with distinction and twelve with commendations; ten had to resit. Seven postgraduates passed. The external examiners were 'greatly impressed by the College's endeavours'. But the Principal pinpointed two problems: getting academic and professional standards established and enabling the staff (many of whom were young) to mature in the highly complicated business of training teachers.

5. The Queen Mother opens the College

Michaelmas Term 1967 was in many ways a 'beginning', Dr Pollard said in his final report to Manchester. 'From September we become a member of the University of Lancaster School of Education. Our new course structure ... has been accepted ..., BEd courses

The College Chapel

The central focus of the College chapel is the large slate altar round which gathers the worshipping community, especially to celebrate the eucharist. The building is typical of the 1960s. It was carefully sited near the entrance to the College to symbolise the central place which Christian belief and worship were intended to have in this new Church college. Light pours down on to the altar from the central tower and the cross cleverly placed in the window of this tower stands out, lit from behind at night as you go up the hill to the College.

The controversial crucifixion scene by John Bratby (died 1992) is behind the altar (see page 17). Another work of the 1960s, it is disturbing to many. It came to the college when it was rejected by a theological hall of residence. The Christ figure in the centre is Bratby himself. It reflects his own neutrality and friends stand on either side, looking away bewildered or unconcerned.

Under the altar are stones from a cave near Tours where St Martin, a fifth-century bishop lived. On two walls are terra-cotta plaques by a local artist, Mabel Pakenham-Walsh, recalling people and places of the Old Testament. The fine organ was built by Peter Collins in 1974 on classical lines which would be familiar to J. S. Bach.

Some furniture was designed by Swedish artists, reflecting the Swedish connection of the College's early years. The only stained glass window is Swedish too—by Einar Forseth. This shows St Martin, riding on his officer's horse and giving half his cloak to a beggar. It is in a small side chapel used for groups wanting to reflect in more intimate surroundings.

For the first ten years chaplains were provided by members of the Society of the Sacred Mission and Professor Dent used to say that S Martin's was eccentric 'with its Swedes and its monks'.

The chapel is in daily use for worship. Since the College began, an hour is timetabled in the middle of the week for a college service. At first it was a eucharist, but now there are services of many traditions, reflecting the greater co-operation between churches and a wide range of church music.

Chaplains

(Until 1974, they were supplied by the Society of the Sacred Mission, Kelham.)

1964-66	Nigel Kinsella
1966-67	Martin Shaw
1968-70	Austin Masters
1970-73	Edmund Wheat
1973-74	Gordon Holroyd
1974-78	Peter Grime
1978-82	Michael Ainsworth
1982-86	Ian Robins
1986-90	Graham Pollitt

Official opening. From left to right: Bishop Claxton, the Queen Mother and Dr Pollard.
(Lancaster Guardian)

have been agreed upon and our Post Graduate Department has increased to thirty five.' (The Certificate entry was the highest ever—193—giving a total of 525 students and 52 staff.) A lively prospectus was produced (destined to last until 1974).

But a great preoccupation was the Official Opening on 16 November by Queen Elizabeth, the Queen Mother. Preparations were meticulous. Speeches were vetted—even Bishop Claxton was firmly limited to three minutes. Gowns—and episcopal gaiters—

were worn, but not Scholl's sandals even if they were the fashion. All were warned to address her as 'Ma'am to rhyme with pram'. So the great day came, the Queen Mother progressed through the college with her usual charm—and as usual ran late. The Archbishop of York was deputed to speed her on to her next engagement. 'Goodbye, Ma'am,' he said. 'Oh, are you going?' HM enquired. 'No, Ma'am, you are,' came the reply!

S Martin's was launched.

4

Consolidation (1967–71)

The four years from 1967 to 1971 were fundamentally a time of consolidation for the 3–4 year course while the College came to terms with a rapidly increasing PGCE intake. In-service work slowly developed and the boldness of the University in instituting an Honours BEd for serving teachers in 1970 provided a splendid opportunity to extend relationships with the schools and the teacher students became a valued element in the College as they worked alongside fourth year students.

In 1968 the Department of Education and Science [DES] for a time pressed for S Martin's to contribute to the continuing national expansion which was still causing new colleges to be founded. It suggested taking over accommodation at St Leonard's House (formerly Waring and Gillow's furniture workshops in the City) which the University was expected to vacate soon. Hugh Harding, Under Secretary in the DES in charge of Teacher Training who was to achieve the reputation within a few short years of a twentieth century Thomas Cromwell (Seaman, p. 109), mentioned a figure of 1,000 students as a minimum for a college to avoid being a 'Cinderella' in the 1970s. After lengthy discussions, the college reluctantly agreed 'not to oppose' such a plan in spite of apprehensions about a larger college—working on split sites and losing its ethos. Then the accommodation proved not to be available after all, and by June 1969 the DES limited the college to 730 and refused to add PE and Drama to the main subjects. In 1970 only one permanent appointment was made—to replace Ruth-Mary Walker who had been promoted to be Vice Principal of Darlington College.

Increasing overall numbers led to great pressure on space. In fact two houses in the city were leased and named Rhodes House after the Lord Lieutenant, Lord Rhodes. This offsite accommodation was useful but, as expected, unpopular and was later abandoned to become a Teachers' Centre. The construction of four lecture rooms in Field Head and eighteen staff studies in the 'Backs' and the rebuilt miniature rifle range proved invaluable and plans were discussed for a new library.

Pressure on teaching practice places grew inexorably—230 students were out in the summer of 1968—so some first year primary students went to Argyll (long retaining idyllic memories of small rural schools) while Post Graduate Certificate in Education [PGCE] secondary students exploited the tougher situations of Glasgow and Lanarkshire.

For the PGCE course was rapidly expanded from 10 in 1965 to 184 in 1971. Jim Garbett took it over in 1968 and developed a secondary course pattern which stood the test of time. The core was a first subject course usually led by a Tutor who also acted as the students' personal/professional tutor. This, with a one term's second subject course, (including a very successful Outdoor Pursuits course), occupied about half the time in College, the concentration being on preparing students to be effective in the classroom. The Lent Term was spent on teaching practice. The other half of college time was spent on relevant educational theory (with some choice in the summer term) intended to help the student to look wider. A Primary course developed for 20 plus students, but at this period fewer graduates saw primary teaching

Students socialising.

as a suitable profession than was the case in the 1980s. Quite a high proportion of staff was involved in the PGCE which provided an interesting expansion of their work. Lancaster graduates never provided more than half the intake and usually over thirty institutions of higher education were represented. Most had good honours degrees. From the start the anxiety lest there should be ill-feeling between PGCE and Certificate students largely proved unjustified and the Graduate Course Consultative Committee was an invaluable 'feedback' mechanism. But over the years Bishop Bulley's comment proved correct. The nature of the course—taken almost entirely by day students—meant that graduates did not have the time or opportunity to be much involved in College activities except for sports, chapel (in a few cases) and (while it ran) the Music course which recruited some outstanding organists.

Coping with argumentative graduates was one aspect of a development of the late 1960s—student demands to be involved in the management of institutions. The 'age of majority' had been lowered to eighteen in Britain in 1969. In Western Europe students expressed deep dissatisfaction with the higher education system, sometimes erupting into violence. Inevitably, at S Martin's—as in other residential colleges—expansion with higher numbers of day students affected the corporate ethos but care had been taken to try to maintain good relationships. Besides the staff-student committee, and the tutorial system, each Department had its Consultative Committee. However, students felt they should have a place on the supreme committees. In 1969 the Governors agreed that three students should be elected (not co-opted) on to the Governing body. Procedures were also set up to democratise college disciplinary

The Social Bar.

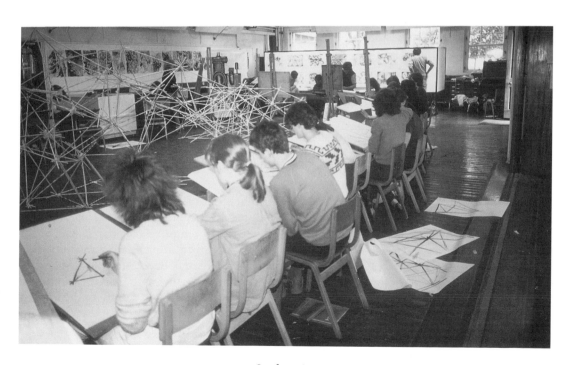

Student Art.

Outdoor Pursuits.

result of his parsimony was that the college became increasingly under-funded in the 1980s when increases in grant were calculated in percentage terms.

Student independence showed itself more—as Dr Owen pointed out to the Governors in her farewell report to them before leaving to become Principal of St Mary's College, Cheltenham, in 1970. She also criticised the great burden of work on students and their inability to experiment. This was echoed by her successor, Margaret Wallis (from Coventry College), six months later. Birman Nottingham, a priest psychologist, who had become Tutor in charge of BEd fourth year students, had also pointed to the particularly onerous demands of this year, not surprising when the new degree had to demonstrate its Honours quality by producing good results (mostly second class degrees with only a few thirds) but nonetheless very hard on students. So staff were led to look more critically at the curriculum and changes began to be made to primary method courses.

procedures. The Academic Board eventually admitted student members in 1971. Staff's anxieties proved groundless; often students were lost in the academic minutiae but at times they made valuable contributions.

The Governors supported students in other ways. They paid half the salary of a sabbatical President from 1969 since student life was so active (except politically) and, as the need for a new Student Common Room became evident, the Governors financed an entirely new building. This was opened on S Martin's Day 1970—by the Archbishop of York—and with the staff/student social bar fostered student social life. The Governors' ability to do this—and steadily to repay central Church funds for the money spent on establishing the college—was due to the College's growing reputation as a conference centre (which increased private funds) and the shrewdness of the Bursar. A less fortunate

This was appropriate because once more, especially after the Plowden Report criticised primary courses, criticisms of the teacher training system became vocal. This provoked three public enquiries in rapid succession which involved inordinate meetings. The teacher training colleges were destined at last to become unequivocally part of the higher education system but at a cost: loss of identity as a separate sector, drastic cuts and many personal tragedies. However, S Martin's, by luck and prudent management, survived.

5

'Education—a framework for expansion'? (1970–3)

1. *National enquiries into teacher training*

The 1960s was a decade which made remarkable demands upon the teacher training system: expansion in size, academic and professional enhancement and administrative reorganisation all had to be tackled simultaneously. The new decade did not, however, promise that period of calm which the system required if it was to consolidate itself after the radical changes of the 1960s. Training institutions have never been without their critics and by the late 1960s the volume of criticism was such that in February 1970 the then Secretary of State [Edward Short] asked the University Area Training Organisations, which at that time still had responsibility for the award of all initial teacher qualifications, to review college courses. (McNamara and Ross, 1982, p. 2)

Typically Hugh Pollard—who always felt it was his duty to keep staff well informed—circulated Short's letter to all the staff within two weeks of its being sent to Vice Chancellors. It raised again questions about the theoretical underpinning of initial teacher education and the adequacy of the practical training which continued to exercise thinking to the 1990s—the possibility of new patterns of training, the relevance of the traditional academic subjects to teachers of young children, teaching practice and the involvement of teachers, the adequacy of the course in relation to practical teaching problems.

Evidence presented to the House of Commons Select Committee of 1969–70 included compliments to the system for what had been achieved in the 1960s. In less than twenty years there had been a 440 per cent increase in the number of students, resulting in 110,000 students on three-year courses in 165 colleges in 1970 (Stewart, 1989, p. 74), which also reinforced the case being made for an enquiry. This was set up by Mrs Margaret Thatcher in the first year of the new Conservative administration late in 1970 when, as Secretary of State, she appointed a group under Lord James to make recommendations quickly on what should be the content and organisation of teacher education courses, whether some students should be educated with non-teachers, and what the role of the types of higher education institution should be.

One fundamental issue was the place of teacher education colleges in the higher education system. In 1960 they were still a significant separate sector of post-secondary education. But with the rapid expansion after the Robbins Report (1963) and the creation of the 'binary' system of university and 'public' sectors when thirty polytechnics were designated in 1966, the survival of the colleges as a 'third force' became increasingly questioned. The Secretary of State, Anthony Crosland, in his famous speech at Woolwich which led to the setting up of the binary system, had included the colleges of education in the public sector. The significance of this was to become clearer as the 1970s advanced. The colleges themselves in 1970 had raised the possibility of diversification into arts degrees and the 'caring professions'. Moreover, applications for Certificate of Education courses began to fall in numbers and quality (though not at S Martin's), students became more reluctant to take a course which committed them to one career only, and the colleges were still felt to be isolated and academically inferior. Then Department of Education and Science [DES] officials began to show awareness of demographic trends. The Under Secretary, Hugh Harding, pointed out to a conference of all college principals in 1970 that the birth rate was not rising again as expected after its recent fall and too many teachers were being produced.

2. A new relationship with the University of Lancaster?

Against this background, although S Martin's was fast settling into a routine of admitting annually over 300 students for the three-year Certificate and one-year Post Graduate Certificate in Education [PGCE] courses, staff began discussing future developments in a series of Academic Board meetings from as early as February 1970. In October, a group suggested that the College should build on its academic strengths and rising quality of students by admitting students from 1973 for a four-year BEd (Honours) course only. Subsequent meetings showed the staff to be in favour of developing this into a wider programme of courses whilst retaining teacher training as the primary focus. This was a first tentative move away from being a 'monotechnic'.

Difficult issues were raised: recognition of staff by the University for BA teaching, increase in size to over 1000 students, a different relationship with the University whilst retaining the College's Christian ethos. This last issue was to provoke a great deal of discussion over the next few years.

Teaching degree courses and a close relationship with the University of Lancaster had

been in Dr Pollard's mind from the beginning. In 1970–1, with the encouragement of Mr Hugh Harding he began to investigate the possibility of the College's putting on non-teaching degrees and establishing a new relationship with its neighbouring university as an experiment. The College of St John at York had made a similar request to York University, for discussions, started in 1967, to be reopened (McGregor, 1991, p. 196). As a voluntary Church College with direct access to the DES and its own funding arrangements, S Martin's had greater freedom for manoeuvre than a college controlled by any LEA. Dr Pollard was also encouraged by Canon James Robertson, who was establishing himself rapidly as an authoritative Secretary to the Council of Church Colleges. He already was raising the notion of the Church Colleges federating to form a degree-awarding university but as another Principal commented, the vision 'was, alas! to pass away because each of the Church colleges was too engrossed with its immediate and complex negotiations with its own university, concerning the next stage of development.' (Rose, 1981, p. 114)

Dr Pollard selected four senior staff to help in this investigation. Among those consulted were Professor Harold Dent and the Heads of two Catholic Colleges. The Vice-Chancellor also supported the idea—but prudently raised problems which eventually proved insurmountable. The discussions had to include other colleges within the ATO as the University could not be seen to be negotiating with only one—especially when that College was denominational and the University's Charter specifically forbade any test related to 'religious, moral or political belief'. Yet Mr Carter did not favour any scheme which might threaten S Martin's strengths and Christian ethos. A series of discussions ensued and the Senate sympathetically debated the matter of having 'associated colleges' in the first half of 1972. But as Marion McClintock put it in her history of the University (1974, p. 188), 'the idea of association with the colleges … fell away'.

The James Report on teacher education was published in February 1972. It advocated three 'cycles' of education for teachers: personal education, pre-service training leading to a degree followed by an induction year, and a greatly expanded provision for in-service training. A two-year Diploma in Higher Education to be taken in colleges and polytechnics was proposed and the Report expressed the hope 'that the voluntary bodies would agree to a widening of functions for their colleges'. A majority on the Commission proposed replacing the current Area Training Organisations based on universities with Regional Councils. A government White Paper on the future of higher education was expected to follow quickly.

This duly appeared in December 1972 ironically under the title *Education: a framework for expansion*. It inaugurated a decade in which 'the government undertook the largest and most controversial reorganisation of higher education that there has ever been in England and Wales.' (Locke, 1985, p. 1) Expansion was certainly planned for higher education in general, but there was an abrupt change of policy about the colleges of education. 'Among staff in the colleges the White Paper was soon dubbed "A Frame-up for Contraction".' (McGregor, 1991, p. 201) Numbers of initial training places required by 1981 were reduced to 60–70,000 compared with the 1971-72 figure of about 114,000, although the equivalent of another 15,000 places would be needed for the in-service work strongly recommended by James. But radical changes in the role and status of the colleges of education were forecast as their functions were to be substantially broadened from being 'monotechnics'. Some might combine with neighbouring institutions, some might be 'integrated' with universities, 'some may need to close'; ie, the colleges were no longer to continue as a distinguishable third sector. 'Difficult problems of organisation and finance will be involved' and 'staffs must face major changes'. Assimilation or mergers of colleges with larger institutions (usually polytechnics) was clearly the preferred solution and 'economies of scale' (never defined) became a major principle in the ensuing re-organisation.

This prompted a brief resumption of high level discussions between S Martin's and the University. The College presented seven 'tests for real autonomy as a College of the University' (supported interestingly by an independent memorandum from the students' union). But by March 1973 it became quite clear that the University—and the University Grants Committee—would accept only a very strong definition of 'integration' so the College rejected this loss of independence.

In fact, the College had been making tentative enquiries to see if some association with the Council for National Academic Awards [CNAA] (the path chosen by many colleges subsequently) or the Open University might prove more advantageous, but in the event the existing relationship with the University through the School of Education was maintained. This became easier over the years as the University gained in reputation and self confidence and the College demonstrated its quality.

3. *Academic developments*

Meanwhile the College was working hard at the task of providing worthwhile courses to more than 700 students. Certificate students, following the national trend to some extent, declined slightly and (reflecting the long standing shortage of science teachers) Physics and Chemistry were not offered as main subjects after 1973. But the quality of entry rose until already in 1972 63 per cent of the men and 59 per cent of the women had two or three A-levels (against the national averages of 39 and 41 per cent respectively). The fourth BEd year increased only slowly (see Appendix), though the group was augmented and enriched by seconded teachers studying for their in-service BEd degree, one of Professor Alec Ross' innovations.

Smarties have the answer!

PGCE targets, however, rose to 180 by 1971 and stayed at that figure until the 'Secondary' cuts of the 1980s. Noteworthy developments included a popular integrated Science Education course, introduced in 1973, and recruiting young priests from Kelham Theological College for 'Post ordination training' as RE teachers. David Urwin developed the Education side and the Primary course settled down when Elizabeth Green took charge of it in 1973. Particularly pleasing was the complimentary report on the PGCE courses by Darlow Humphreys, formerly Head of the Bristol PGCE course, when he was the external examiner for S Martin's.

In the three- and four-year course, four elements were now identified nationally—academic studies, theory of education, professional studies and teaching practice. Education studies were based on the four 'disciplines' which had become fashionable—history, philosophy, psychology and sociology—but S Martin's was distinctive in ensuring, as a Church college, that all students thought about the value issues raised through philosophy.

Working out useful professional studies courses to prepare students for the classroom continued to exercise the college. The Junior/Secondary course, purporting to cover the 7 to 16 age range, proved unsatisfactory so in 1972, three age-range courses were introduced: First school (5 to 8), Middle Years (8 to 13) and Secondary (11 to 16) since Certificate students were still acceptable as secondary school teachers. The range of subjects covered grew steadily (as did student contact time) anticipating the National Curriculum of the late 1980s. Noteworthy were the development of French and the place of RE taken by all primary students (including PGCE students) on the grounds that no child's education was complete if RE (as distinct from Christian education) was not taught. An unusual success was the teaching of a Mathematical Education course jointly to BEd and University third year students and European Studies were introduced into the College curriculum from 1975.

In 1973 Bill Etherington was appointed Principal of Keswick Hall College of Education, Norwich and David Naylor left to become famous as RE Adviser for Hampshire. Bill was succeeded by Jim Garbett. In an attempt to strengthen Professional Studies in the Certificate a separate Division was created under Peter Gedge in 1975. He set up three age range Committees and a lasting framework of courses. However an HMI inspection in May criticised this separation from educational studies and the experiment lasted only one year, although the Academic Board did say that through the Division members 'had seen a new unity and cohesion in Professional courses'.

4. Deans

Another reorganisation, however, was longer lasting. As part of the assimilation of the training colleges into the Public Sector of Higher Education [PSHE], the 1974 Houghton Report had made recommendations about pay scales. Regulations put colleges under the same grading structure as Further Education colleges and polytechnics. This made staff salaries dependent now on 'unit totals' computed from the numbers of hours taught, the total of students taking a course and the academic level of work. Heads of Department posts were to be introduced (based on the grades of their departments) on the same basis as in Further Education. Jean Murray (former Principal of Mather College, Manchester) had been brought by Dr Pollard out of retirement to lead the First School Committee and she was entrusted with calculating how the new regulations affected the college given its size and range of work. A working party of governors and staff then investigated (again) College organisation. The result was the introduction from 1 January 1976 of a new Faculty structure. Because the College could afford (only) three Heads of Department, teaching was divided into three areas—Educational and Professional, Postgraduate, and Academic Studies—each under a Dean, Jim Garbett, Barry Ogden and Peter Gedge. The Heads of Academic Subjects formed a team whose pre-eminence was now clearly reduced, not merely by the introduction of Deans but by the creation of 'Heads of Area' in the other two Faculties as part of the process of raising appropriately the status of Educational and Professional Studies within the College. As a member of staff who had studied the changes as part of his MA course put it, a restructuring involving pay had been responsible for a complete redistribution of power within the college.

Unsurprisingly there was some opposition but the Governors confirmed the new system, staff accepted it, and it was made to work. Undoubtedly many junior staff felt the new system was unduly bureaucratic. In-Service Education and Training (INSET) was a major new development. Occasional courses had been mounted for some years. But the James Report and the White Paper insisted on the importance of INSET and under the forceful leadership of Tony James great progress was made soon resulting in the annual recruitment of over 150 'full time equivalent' (fte) students. Good relationships were developed with local authorities which would prove important in the future fight to survive. In 1975 the first Advanced Certificates and Diplomas in Advanced Studies in Education (DASE) were validated by the University and accepted by the DES. Barry Gregson's renowned one-term clay course started a long run. Other notable achievements were the one-term Teacher Fellowship and the introduction in 1976 (with the support of Professor Ninian Smart) of the MA in RE, which recruited some interesting overseas students.

Pressure on staff was exacerbated by the determined policy of seconding staff to acquire further qualifications. But the results paid off. Even by 1973, when most colleges had a high proportion of non-graduate lecturers, 87 per cent of the staff were graduates (including an increasing number of Primary education staff) and 42 per cent had higher degrees. In 1975, HMI commented that they considered the staff of the College were the best qualified they had found in colleges of education.

5. More buildings

Pressure on buildings was exacerbated too, as the total of students remained well over 700, but through Dr Pollard's fund-raising and the Bursar's thrift, accommodation steadily grew. Harold Bridges gave £16,000 towards the College's share of the cost of a new library, opened by the famous actress Dame Flora Robson in 1975. The old library in the Keep was converted into a Resources Centre and an Audio-Visual Aids Centre was set up. More lecture rooms were built in 1976 named after Bishop Martineau who had become Chairman of Governors when Bishop Claxton retired in 1971, leaving a fine gate named in honour of him. Facilities in the Art department were extended and College funds paid for an all-weather illuminated pitch which was a great asset to the College and wider community.

6. Life outside the classroom

When Bill Etherington addressed the governors before moving in 1973 he commented that personal relationships in S Martin's were better than at most colleges because of tutorial groups and the Consultative Committee system. Probably this was why the College largely escaped the student unrest so widespread in this period.

Charities were regularly supported through Rag Weeks. Dramatic performances ranged from *Measure for Measure* to pantomimes, one being especially memorable for the performance of Red Riding Hood's Grandmother, alias Father Edmund Wheat. As a very successful College chaplain from 1970 to 1973, he ensured that the Chapel continued to be significant in the life of staff and students, notably through the Thursday midday College Eucharist. The Chapel Choir maintained a high standard under Peter Moore, who was delighted by the Governors' gift of a fine Collins classical organ in 1974. The College Choir gave two concerts annually in College and sang in four cathedrals. There was an interesting series of French and German carol services. From 1976 the College provided premises for the new Haffner Orchestra, typical of its offering facilities readily to the local community. In spite of a shortage of male students, a good range of team games for both sexes was maintained with success.

Dr Pollard's policy of occasional first-rate entertainment was continued too. Joyce

Harold Bridges Library.

Grenfell came in 1970, Elisabeth Söderström sang lieder in 1972, Noel Rawsthorne (Liverpool Cathedral) gave a recital on the new organ in 1975 and Flora Robson returned in 1976.

View across the square.

Dr Pollard's last years, (1973–6)

1. *Colleges in crisis:* 1973–6

While the College was quietly getting on with its job, what David Hencke (1978), in his lively book *Colleges in Crisis*, called 'the drift through chaos policy, 1973–6' was affecting the teacher training sector. The White Paper had foreshadowed changes. In July 1973 Circular 7/73 began the implementation of the policy—'a major consideration of the future role of colleges of education both in and outside teacher training'. Hencke considered that 'the three years that followed the publication of Circular 7/73 were marked by total confusion for all the participants with the possible exception of [DES] officials' (p. 56). Their primary aim remained to build up a larger and more unified sector of local authority higher education (Sharp, 1987) and the prospect for most colleges of education was much closer assimilation into the non-university sector of higher education. But one fact became increasingly clear. The Department was determined to reduce the number of teachers in training in the 1980s from the 1971–2 figure of about 114,000. The target fell in stages until November 1976 when the low figure of 45,000 was proposed, comprising 10,000 'full time equivalent' in-service students, 5000 on PGCE courses and only 30,000 BEd or Certificate students.

The sector was disrupted for several years after the White Paper as institutions fought for survival—retaining an independent identity if possible. But the number of colleges was reduced by 1982 to a third of the total ten years earlier. Hencke's verdict was very critical. 'Since 1972 the government has had a golden opportunity to reform the system.

That it has failed is appalling enough. But to fail and disrupt an entire academic system is unforgivable.' (p. 123) Great was the toll on staff as careers were disrupted—or ended by redundancy though the terms of the Crombie Code made this easier to endure from 1975. This code provided quite generous terms of compensation for staff made redundant when intakes to colleges were reduced by the Secretary of State or colleges were closed.

The twenty-seven Church Colleges had at least one advantage over the fragmented LEA colleges: they were a coherent group which already had a tradition of group consultation and response to national pressures. This group identity had been carefully fostered by Canon Robertson, Secretary until 1974. Consequently, although the Church of England had little effective power against the DES which controlled college finance and student intakes, nevertheless it established a claim to an 'historic share' of the revised figures. It was, however, a sign of the times that the Church, which had dominated teacher training until well into the twentieth century, could now claim as its 'historic share' only one-sixth, and that included numbers of students absorbed into universities. The Church could, therefore, through its Conferences of Principals, retain some initiative in allocating places among the surviving Church colleges, but there was a fatal weakness typical of Anglican institutions. A General Synod paper declared that the Colleges were 'a confederation of autonomous institutions linked by common purposes...' They were 'not branches of a centrally directed enterprise.' (GS 194, Misc.) Canon Robertson's departure in 1974 worsened the situation and the

Church of England Colleges, 1974–90

CLOSED:
- Culham College, Abingdon
- Hockerill College
- St Gabriel's College, London
- St Peter's College, Saltley
- Sarum St Michael College

SUBSUMED:

All Saints College, Tottenham	Middlesex Polytechnic
College of the Venerable Bede, Durham	merged with St Hild's College, then subsumed in University
Keswick Hall College, Norwich	subsumed in University
St Gabriel's College, London	Goldsmith's College, London University
St Hild's College, Durham	merged with Bede College, then subsumed in University
St Luke's College, Exeter	subsumed in University
St Mary's College, Bangor	subsumed in Bangor Normal College
St Matthias College, Bristol	subsumed in Bristol Polytechnic

MERGERS/FEDERATIONS acknowledging Church of England element:

Bishop Lonsdale College, Derby	merged with Derby College of Technology into Derby Lonsdale, then with Matlock College as **Derbyshire College**
Bishop Otter College, Chichester	merged with Bognor Regis College into **West Sussex Institute of Higher Education**
St Katharine's College, Liverpool	federated with Christ's and Notre Dame as **Liverpool Institute of Higher Education**
Whitelands College, London	federated with Southlands, Digby Stuart and Froebel as **Roehampton Institute of Higher Education**

FREESTANDING:

Bishop Grosseteste College, Lincoln	monotechnic
Chester College	diversified
Christ Church College, Canterbury	diversified
College of St Mark and St John, Plymouth	diversified
King Alfred's College, Winchester	diversified
Ripon College	merged with St John's College, York as College of Ripon and York St John, diversified
St John's College, York	merged with Ripon College as College of Ripon and York St John, diversified
S Martin's College, Lancaster	diversified
St Mary's College, Cheltenham	merged with St Paul's College as **College of St Paul and St Mary**, diversified
St Paul's College, Cheltenham	merged with St Mary's College as College of St Paul and St Mary, diversified
Trinity College, Carmarthen	diversified

Church colleges suffered from a lack of firm central leadership. This was a great change from the 1960s when policy was led by Bishop Stopford (London) as Chairman of the Board of Education and Bishop Claxton (Blackburn) as Chairman of the Council of Church Colleges of Education. As Dr Pollard said to the Academic Board, closure and amalgamation presented 'a confusing and sad prospect for many Church colleges'.

This was only too well illustrated by a difficult Conference of Church College Principals held at York in 1975. In the end only nine of the twenty-seven Church colleges remained free standing (see box). S Martin's was one, though at the final announcement in 1977 it lost fifty teacher training places to Cheltenham whose lobbying had proved to be more effective. Why was it lucky when some excellent ancient colleges disappeared? Regional position was one argument. Hopefully, quality was another. In October 1974 Mr Harding had told the Lancashire Chief Education Officer, Percy Lord, that S Martin's should survive but even a year later he said (obscurely) that he would like the relationship with the University of Lancaster established 'on a more secure basis'. However, in spite of further attempts by the Vice-Chancellor and the University secretary, Stephen Jeffreys, to work out some acceptable form of affiliation, S Martin's remained a 'free-standing' institution.

2. A new BEd course

Planning for a new BEd degree scheme had restarted in 1973 after the White Paper. Despite some misgivings about excluding able teachers lacking in academic qualifications, the notion of terminating the Certificate course had been soon accepted (anticipating the Government's decision to do this from 1980). Much thought was devoted to devising a complex modular Honours/Ordinary degree scheme to start in 1975. This would have added courses leading to the Diploma in

Higher Education advocated by the James Report and to a BA degree oriented towards the caring professions for students who did not want to be teachers. To be different from the University, 'inter-disciplinary' courses were devised. University staff were consulted and an impressive volume set out this modular scheme which would have made much wider student choice of units possible. But at a University meeting in March 1974 disaster struck: the scheme was rejected as lacking proper coherence and progression; a more sequential approach was called for. Not until the 1990s were modular schemes accepted.

It was to the credit of the College—and the University—that a rapid salvage operation, led by the Vice-Principal, produced in the same summer an outline BEd scheme introduced in 1975 as planned. Students took a main subject through three or four years. Professional Studies was now to be assessed in the same way as any 'academic' subject illustrating the important advances being made nationally in the colleges towards defining what was meant by a professional degree. (McNamara and Ross, 1982, p. 40) Students could qualify for entry to Part II Honours after two years (or leave then with the Diploma in Higher Education—though hardly anyone did). This removed the unsatisfactory pattern of adding a very heavy BEd fourth year to a Certificate course. A BEd (Ordinary) degree was available at the end of Year 3 for those who did not qualify for Honours or preferred—as some did initially—to leave after three years.

An interesting variant was the Community and Youth Studies course. This included experience in both schools and community situations and produced teachers who also had a community and youth work qualification until the DES stopped such courses in 1987. The foundations were laid for what became a strong independent department in the later 1980s and the students regularly made significant contributions to College and union activities.

This replacement for the Certificate course came at a very opportune time for the College and Mr Harding was impressed on his visit in October 1975 to hear that (against the national trend) with a target of 150 the College had recruited 133 students with at least two passes at Advanced level. This degree scheme illustrates the 1970s' move towards an all-graduate teaching profession. However, the traditional distinction between primary/elementary and secondary teachers still remained as the BEd developed into a qualification for primary teachers only.

3. Dr Pollard retires

In November 1975, Ernest Helm retired as Bursar, having achieved a national reputation. He was replaced by Paul Winter. Helm had the satisfaction of completing the repayment to the Central Board of Finance of £150,000 towards the £298,536 paid by the Church of England as its share of the capital costs of founding the College, 1964–69. During his time annual estimates had increased tenfold and were now approaching one million pounds.

Dr Pollard also announced he would retire at the end of that academic year, although he was only sixty-one. He had achieved much. A derelict barracks had been converted to a pleasant campus. A substantial sum had been repaid to the Church and many gifts attracted. At a time when many colleges were facing closure or amalgamation, the College had grown to more than 700 students with an active Students' Union, a real sense of a caring community and sound staff-student relationships. Among those who commented on the College's unique atmosphere were such leading educational figures as Sir Percy Lord and Lord Morris (Governor and former vice-chancellor of Leeds University). A distinctive ethos as a church-related institution had been established, with an active Chapel as its focus and the college was seen to be serving the Church. A reputation had been won for solid academic and professional work in preparing teachers and INSET and a new degree course replacing the Certificate of Education had been started. Good relationships existed with the University, local LEAs and the community. Perhaps his greatest achievement was the welding together of the staff, their acceptance of the Christian foundation and their devotion to the future of the College. That certainly was a major factor in its survival and growth over the next decade. He was publicly honoured for his achievements: the Queen made him an OBE, the King of Sweden awarded the Order of the Vasa, the University conferred an LLD (in 1989).

But new challenges lay ahead—further cuts in teacher education and the need to 'diversify' with other courses. At great personal cost, Dr Pollard decided it was time to give way to a Principal with different qualities so in August 1976 he left, typically after a farewell Eucharist attended by six bishops in Lancaster Priory and an entertainment by Dame Flora Robson. His portrait—by Claude Harrison—is highly symbolic. He stands, a lonely figure in full academic dress, in front of the Keep and the Chapel, while in the sky loom wintry grey clouds portending the new storms that lay ahead for his successor—Robert Clayton.

7

A balancing act (1976–81)

1. *The new Principal, Robert Clayton*

Succeeding a Founder-Principal is not easy, especially when that Principal had stamped his personality on the institution and evolved such a distinctive management style. Also, Robert Clayton had served under Dr Pollard at the College of St Mark and St John. However, he had developed the LEA college at Matlock successfully and his forceful style (though abrasive to some) was in many ways well-suited to the 'entrepreneurial' approach required of the college now that Initial Teacher Education no longer had a separate structure and system of administration within higher education but had to fight for courses and students in the 'public' sector of Advanced Further Education. As McGregor (1991, p. 218) put it, 'The Church colleges

now had not just two masters [the Department of Education and Science and the Church Board of Education] but six since support had to be obtained in addition from a university or the CNAA, the LEA, the regional HMI and the Regional Advisory Council for Further Education [RAC]'.

From his first meetings, he made it clear that S Martin's had to become less insular and 'sell itself', and his first priority was, as directed by the White Paper and supported by Dr Pollard, to make up for falling Initial Teacher Education (ITE) numbers. This was to be achieved by 'diversifying', as Mr Harding had said, into 'Liberal Arts' degrees, building on existing strengths to 'rationalise' the use of college resources, avoid staff redundancies and enable ITE students to work alongside others not intending to be teachers. As Locke (1985, p. 102) put it, the key prob-

Robert Clayton

Mr Clayton came to S Martin's College with a high reputation as a teacher, manager and writer. After military service and living in India, he took a degree at the College of St Mark and St John in Chelsea. He taught at Leominster and, on returning to his college, he became Head of Geography and Vice-Principal. He wrote textbooks and became an authority on London. He was appointed to S Martin's after a successful period as Principal at Matlock College in Derbyshire. He was also a magistrate there. Like Dr Pollard, he was a very cultured man, with skills as pianist and painter, and had a good rapport with students. He served on a number of committees and was Chairman of the Society for Research in Higher Education. His wife, Rose, was a talented fashion designer.

lem was to identify growth areas and recruit students within the administrative constraints, notably the constraints in public expenditure after the 1973 oil crisis. So he gave greater impetus to the policy of establishing BA courses and slowly the range of options and student target numbers increased. This, with the further development of in-service courses, kept student numbers above 670 at a time when many places were amalgamating or closing and laid the foundations for marked growth in the 1980s.

2. *Diversification into Arts BA degrees*

The Lancaster pattern of BA degree course was adopted with its three-subject one-year Part I and two-subject Part II. Five BA (Honours) schemes (including a subject unique in England—Social Ethics) were put up to the Regional Advisory Council via the Regional Staff Inspector who emerged as a powerful figure.

Brian Gates' appointment as Head of Religious Studies produced this added bonus. He had studied the subject in the USA and suggested it to Dr Pollard. It was felt to be a highly appropriate subject for a Church college since it aimed to provide an opportunity for studying the key area of values in contemporary society through a systematic study of the grounds and criteria for ethical action and their application in relation to key issues presently confronting mankind.

The Regional Advisory Council (RAC), which had been set up to rationalise provision of courses in the north west, after some delays accepted this argument and the case for a degree in English. Mr Clayton took these proposals to the University which had major anxieties about the quality of BA courses being proposed in the colleges. While College staff and resources had proved acceptable for teaching BEd (Hons) subject studies, teaching Lancaster BA (Hons) degrees was felt to involve a major step to something new. Nor

should students be admitted with too low Advanced level qualifications.

However, fundamentally, the University was sympathetic and, by 1978, using its rigorous, if sometimes lengthy, procedures the two BA (Hons) schemes were validated. The key conditions were the appointment of some new staff and students had to have at least two A-level passes at grade C. The University did not insist, as, for example, Leeds did, on a three-year Part II for an Honours degree in its associated colleges.

Only nineteen students were admitted in 1978 but the English degree soon found no difficulty in recruiting sound, even some very able, students. Social Ethics, as a new subject, took rather longer to establish itself in terms of quality as measured by A-level grades, but it brought unusual students into College, with a higher proportion of 'mature' and/or 'non-standard' entry students. It was unfortunate that the College was in an area of fairly low population so that there was no large 'pool' of mature students to draw on locally.

The Principal continued his battles with the RAC system and slowly the range grew as the College exploited the DES ruling that a new course could be permitted only if it could be put on 'within existing resources'. A BA (Ordinary) degree was allowed for twenty-four students to take Geography or History in 1980. Units were taught in common where possible to BA and BEd students which usually produced the 'viable' groups (ie at least twelve) on which the RAC insisted. By judicious juggling and slight over-recruiting, from 1982 about 90 BA students were admitted annually. The College student total therefore reached 746 by 1981 and rose steadily thereafter. Staff-student ratios remained acceptable to the DES, ie they deteriorated steadily from 1:10 towards 1:12.

One problem was distinguishing Ordinary from Honours students after Part I. Initially, University Assessors who were the final arbiters were cautious, but the numbers deemed to have qualified for Honours rose steadily and the Ordinary degree died out by 1988 without reducing the level of Honours degrees awarded. Thirds and Firsts remained rare; Pass degrees and Fails were virtually unknown.

3. *Putting the College 'on the map'*

One tactic promoted by Mr Clayton for making the College more widely known was the establishment of Institutes or Centres and the attraction of projects and interesting characters to the college, often primed by College private funds.

The Institute of European Education was one example. David Peacock exploited schools' interest in European Studies in Dr Pollard's last year. In 1978 he set up an Institute, aided by European Commission funds, with a library. Using one of the Job Creation Project teams set up to combat unemployment he created materials for schools in co-operation with teachers. A publicity coup was getting it opened by the former Prime Minister, Edward Heath. The Institute then pioneered Graded Language Tests in Lancashire and Cumbria and extended them to parents, laying the foundations for what developed into a significant area of College enterprise.

A Language and Reading Centre was set up. In 1979, Brian Gates secured the co-operation of the Social Morality Council and DES funding to establish a National Moral Education Centre which produced a useful series of 'Brown Papers'. A British Council of Churches Project based in College produced in 1980 a report on *Young people in the Church*. The Project Officer spent the following year on a pilot piece of research into the self-image of the Church Colleges. This developed into the Culham College Institute's important research, organised by John Gay (1986), into the role of the Church Colleges.

Dave Hicks was given a base in 1980 for a Centre for Peace Studies sponsored by the Schools Council and Joseph Rowntree Trust.

This produced useful books and resources for schools, but also brought on to the College the charge from right wing politicians of supporting a neo-Marxist organisation.

Robert Clayton himself led the College to support his former college, St Mark and St John, in developing the signficant Urban Studies Centre in the east end of London. Progress owed much to his drive and enthusiasm and soon a consortium of four Church colleges was formed to manage it. A significant number of BEd and PGCE students based there had invaluable experience of inner city multi-ethnic school and community placements and many found jobs there afterwards. This project was not cheap but drew favourable comment from HMI and the Church of England's report, *Faith in the City*.

Another ploy was to have lecturers who held joint appointments. So Liz Ramsey came from the Schools Council RE Project to lecture as well as work for the Christian Education Movement, Lancashire LEA and the Anglican Diocese of Blackburn. Andy Smith was seconded half-time to the Health Education Council from 1981 and developed into a tutor with a national reputation for counselling and Active Tutorial Work in secondary schools.

Foreign contacts were encouraged. A growing number of students from the continent visited the College, some to take courses, and a link was built up with the Southern Connecticut State University. A group went to Hungary to experience the Kodaly method of music teaching.

College life was further enriched, and links with schools and FE colleges strengthened, by a series of 'fellowships'. A succession of teachers profited from a term's study in College. One of the most notable was a ceramics teacher who had lost an arm in an accident and found that a term in the Art department completed his rehabilitation.

North West Arts supported Arts Fellows. Clive Hickinbottom came in 1978 with his very distinctive approach to ceramics. He was followed in 1980 by the novelist, Tom Wakefield, who as warden and writer exerted a strong influence, and then by David Cook and Ursula Fanthorpe. Malcolm Wren, as fellow in Religion and the Arts, obtained and organised an outstanding collection of slides to illustrate the teaching of an original BA course. A local dance/drama group 'Ludus' owed much in its early stages to support from the College.

4. *In-service and Adult Education*

Tony James continued to induce staff to see the vital importance of In-Service Education and Training (INSET) for the College both in terms of developing vital relationships with LEAs and schools and increasing numbers of full time equivalent (FTE) students. He was skilful in adapting courses to overcome prob-

Support Staff. From left to right: Allan Baker (Deputy Bursar); Violet Southworth (Housekeeper);
Harry Harrison (Engineer); Paul Winter (Bursar); Gladys Johnson (Deputy Housekeeper).
(Lancaster Guardian)

Mixed hockey.

lems caused by the College's slightly isolated geographical location and by frequent changes in funding arrangements and LEA policy. The Mathematics Department widened its range still further when it was asked in 1977 to introduce a two-year Certificate in Mathematics Teaching as a retraining course financed by the Manpower Services Commission. It continued for several years. A 'College Certificate' was introduced which could be extended into a second year of study leading to a University-validated Advanced Certificate. Another development was consultancy work in schools.

So by 1978, the College approached its target of two-ninths of its work as INSET, claiming 150 FTE students. INSET later became a Faculty and its Co-ordinator was promoted to be the fourth Dean.

Regulations permitting grant aid for what the Regional Staff Inspector described as a 'modest involvement'in adult education were also cleverly exploited to earn further FTEs often in co-operation with Countrywide Holidays Association. One long-lasting part of this work which did much for the College's reputation in the Church at large was the training from 1978 of school governors in close co-operation with the local Anglican Diocese of Blackburn.

5. BEd (Mark 3): rationalisation in action

Initial Teacher Education (ITE) still remained the primary focus of the College and great efforts and ingenuity were needed to continue

Biggles fuels up!

One new requirement was 'substantial' time on the teaching of Mathematics and Language (and from 1980 all ITE candidates, including PGCE students in any subject, had to have a pass at GCSE/GCE 'Ordinary' level in these subjects.) Later Information Technology had to be added and more time found for Science. Not surprisingly a major concern for the College was the workload on Primary students as more and more had to be fitted into the course with no extension of its length. After a quinquennial review a 'Mark 3' BEd was validated for introduction in 1980.

To provide opportunity for BEd students to leave the course early if experience in the first year proved unsatisfying, Part I was largely taught in common with BA students. Most of the second year was devoted to 'Qualificatory' Professional Studies. The theory came in the third year, but, contrary to the later complaint of right wing politicians, it was pruned to a minimum. Also, anticipating later HMI demands, substantial study of one academic subject remained obligatory for Honours Part II students. In most subjects some final year units were taught in common with BA students. This served to provide some options, to create 'viable' groups (ie twelve to fifteen students), to guarantee the academic rigour of the degree and to meet the criticism that 'monotechnic' courses led to ITE students being taught in isolation from other students. A three-year BEd (Ord) for semi-specialists was taught for a short time but it was abandoned as inadequate. This degree

the development of these courses while meeting the increasingly demanding requirements of the DES.

As has been shown, Professional Studies had to cover an ever wider area, largely anticipating what later became the National Curriculum: Mathematics, Language and Reading, Art, Music, Physical Education, Religious and Moral Education, Science, Humanities. The attempts to underpin practice with theory at degree level proved very difficult as the theory remained so contested.

Meanwhile DES/HMI interest in, and control of, the ITE curriculum was growing.

Students relaxing.

scheme was another example of the rational-isation called for by the DES which enabled S Martin's, as a medium-sized college, to survive the acute constraints of 1975-85. This illustrates the general discussion by McNamara and Ross (1982, ch. 1) of the historical background of the BEd degree.

For, as the birth-rate continued to fall, teacher unemployment rose and financial constraints tightened (calling for a 4.7 per cent cut in real terms in 1981 and 7 per cent in 1982-4), so significant further cuts were made in BEd target numbers. Because the BEd became less popular, in 1980 the College could recruit only 70 (its lowest figure ever) for its target of 85. As lower BEd targets were 'directed' by the DES, the College was able to continue to compensate staff declared 're-dundant'. The first three left in 1981. One was

Ben Holgate, Head of Art, who had seen the college obtain a national reputation for the quality of its teaching and work in this field. He had helped both Principals in the steady acquisition of works of art and in organising exhibitions in the Gallery, and his own work had been recently recognised by a commission to make a ceramics Nativity group for the Queen's Royal Chapel of St George, Windsor.

The College Professional Committee forged another valuable link with the profession which was helpful in devising the new BEd. Rather oddly when the government abandoned the system of Area Training Organisations and Institutes of Education in 1975, there was no mechanism for evaluating the professional suitability of ITE courses or their products. So, following a later DES direction, the College set up its own Professional Committee in 1977 with representation from teachers and the Lancashire LEA. The College was itself represented on the similar committee at the University. Teacher members were to supervise the professional aspects of ITE courses and to consider the professional suitability of that year's BEd and PGCE output, very occasionally having to declare that a student should not be allowed to teach.

Teachers were also involved in interviewing students, following DES insistence that the profession must play its part in the selection of students. This was another expression of the feeling that ITE institutions were 'out of touch'. But in fact the profession had always been involved since the College never ignored the school's 'estimate of suitability for teaching' on a candidate's application form.

6. College organisation

Robert Clayton had a less formal style than Dr Pollard and a less explicit way of emphasising the Christian ethos. The practice of starting the year with a College assembly in the Princess Margaretha Hall with the Bishop and Vice-Chancellor ceased, though the first year students still met on their first day to be told that 'perhaps you will end up married to the person you are sitting next to.' A Staff Meeting was held annually (not termly) with an associated Staff Eucharist addressed by a visiting preacher.

He was not comfortable with an Academic Board comprising the entire academic staff, and the pace of change had revealed even in Dr Pollard's time some of the shortcomings of this system. A Working Party had been set up in 1976 to look again at the Board and its committees since Mr Clayton's request had combined with advice from Mr Hugh Harding that a smaller Board was needed in keeping with the recommendations of the Weaver Report. Proposals were made in the summer but the Academic Board and the Governing Body deferred action until the effects of the new faculty structure had been appraised and the new Principal had settled in.

It was therefore not until September 1978 that a smaller Board was set up. Only five members were elected from staff who were not Heads of Subject/Area. Inevitably some members of staff felt diminished and cogs in a bureaucratic system. The Board continued to be 'the policy determining' body with the Principal acting as a very strong Chairman.

However the complex 'political' situation often required quick responses and, as mentioned by the Review Working Party, an 'Advisory' committee emerged in which the Vice Principal and Deans regularly met the Principal to discuss significant issues. Known colloquially as the 'Quintet', it became the 'Sextet' when Tony James was promoted, and finally a 'Septet' when the Bursar became a regular attender.

One issue which concerned staff deeply, as workloads never seemed to lighten, was conditions of service. In 1976 the Colleges' 'trade union', the Association of Teachers in Colleges and Departments of Education, amalgamated with the Association of Teachers in Technical Institutes to form the National Association of Teachers in Further and Higher Education (NATFHE), which seemed to adopt policies more suited to Further Education. Mercifully S Martin's staff were never legalistic and until the mid 1980s there was a large majority of colleagues who had worked together for over ten years. In addition, admirable support was provided on the administrative and domestic side by loyal staff, many of whom worked for the College faithfully for long periods. Consequently staff morale remained generally good, even if the style of management did not please everyone, and most simply got on with whatever needed to be done. The main task of 'management' and the Staffing committee was to try to stop some overworking and to ensure as fair a sharing of burdens as was possible. Other factors were a friendly Senior Common Room and, some would claim, a staff which included a significant number of Christians or people sympathetic to the Christian principles of the College.

This did not mean that the Chaplain's life was easy. Michael Ainsworth, who was Chaplain from 1978 to 1982, told the Governors in 1979 that his task was difficult: congregations were not large and his role was unclear. Nevertheless the Chaplaincy, co-ordinating the efforts of Christians in the College, including a lively Christian Union, played its part, the College service continued its weekly ecumenical act of witness, and local churches, notably St Thomas', Lancaster, developed a valuable complementary ministry to students.

The Students' Union continued its manifold activities with the keen support of Mr Clayton. There was a series of lively committees and hard-working sabbatical Presidents. Care continued to be taken through consultative procedures and the Community Council to produce as many 'satisfied students' as

Sport at S Martin's

Team games soon evolved as one focus for the college spirit. The football team was first trained by the Engineer, Harry Harrison, and an early member, Dave Allison, later achieved national status as a referee. Reaching a high standard was impeded by the low proportion of men students. This was inevitable when the college recruited mainly primary teachers and was prevented by the DES in 1970 from starting a main Physical Education course.

But as the secondary PGCE intake grew, more men were recruited. Games courses were introduced by Peter Jennings and David Bond, first for the graduates and then as BEd options. These were popular, helped students get jobs, and raised standards in the college. The 1980s saw some rugby successes as the new BA degrees brought in some talented players. In the late 1980s fifteen played for the northern colleges and in 1985 a rugby team reached the British Colleges quarter-finals. John Barnes, Andy Hill and Richard Lewthwaite played for British Colleges.

The nearness of the Lake District and Pennines was exploited by students. In 1971 Outdoor Pursuits was added to the list of courses. It led to national awards for mountain leadership, yachting and canoeing. The college was recognised as a centre by the Mountaineering Association. Some great characters were recruited and some went on to careers in the field. Andy Hill featured on TV paddling down the Grand Canyon and from Mount Everest to the sea. Rob Palmer achieved fame as a caver / potholer.

Other games included hockey and women's football, trained for a time by the chaplain, Graham Pollitt. Many women added a Football Referee's Certificate to their portfolio of qualifications.

Gradually the range of sport widened. The large gym was suitable for badminton, and for years staff played on Wednesdays. Innovations in the 1980s included aerobics and fitness testing - and karate attracted some very unlikely students.

The illuminated all-weather pitch, provided in 1971 with the help of a donation from Lord Derby, was invaluable. The college was generous in making facilities available for local organisations when possible.

possible, since they were always the best advertisement for the College and it retained a reputation as a friendly, caring place in which to study.

Inevitably there were changes of personnel. Sir Charles Carter retired as Vice-Chancellor. George Cockburn moved from the School of Education to become Secretary of the University when Stephen Jeffreys, a good friend of the College, retired. He was succeeded first by Stephen Lamley, then by Jim Wood.

7. *The worst is over?*

In 1981 Bishop Martineau chaired his last meeting of the Governing Body before retirement. A new note is clearly detectable in the Principal's report: the worst storms seem to have been weathered—not that the 1980s were to be easy! The BEd tide had turned and the BAs were established. These numbers rose steadily through the 1980s. The PGCE recruited 173, its last such intake for some years as cuts in secondary places were to affect it next. These figures reflected the energetic methods of the Registry. Although the DES steadily provoked the Bursar to utter dire warnings by increasing centralisation and changing procedures at short notice, he still managed to keep expenditure within a few thousand pounds of estimates now totalling well over a million. College private funds continued to grow, largely through income earned by the conference facilities for which the College was becoming famous.

The Government had lacked a clearly published policy when it reorganised teacher training so colleges of education survived in various forms. In 1977 as the 'cuts' were biting, the Church Colleges had reviewed their problems and opportunities at a difficult meeting. Principals spoke of closure (St Peter's, Saltley), coping with reduced ITE targets (King Alfred's, Winchester), federation of colleges (Whitelands), a diversified 'free-standing' college (Chester), and joining a College of Technology (Derby). Under the national pressures all the surviving voluntary colleges formed an Association. In addition to the universities and polytechnics an unexpected 'third force' emerged, marked by the forming in 1977 of SCOPADOC: the Standing Conference of Principals and Directors of Colleges and Institutes of Higher Education. Its first chairman was John Barnett, CBE, who had amalgamated Ripon and York St John's Colleges. So, as Locke (1985) shows, emerged a new form of institution which asserted a distinctive identity and published its own handbook from 1981.

S Martin's was one of the colleges who managed to use 'their historic features to advantage', for example small size, quality of life and religious basis, and exploited their assets to diversify in a fairly conservative way. (Locke, p. 102) By 1981, S Martin's was securely on its way to becoming S Martin's College of Higher Education, although the staff's vision of and support for a distinctively Christian institution had become weaker.

8

The tide turns (1981–8)

1. *Constraints on numbers and finance (NAB and PCFC)*

Constraint not closure was the motif of the 1980s. The College's survival was not in doubt; the major problems were caused by increasing central control since 1972 of the 'public sector' of higher education into which the Church colleges were inexorably drawn. Three trends affected planning. The first was the policy of reducing public spending and dealing with high unemployment, including some unemployment of teachers; demographic trends pointed to a decline in the number of 18-year-olds over the 1980s by one third and the 'age participation rate' (that is, the percentage of this age group entering higher education) was not expected to rise much beyond 14 per cent (in 1985 a fall was even forecast for the late 1990s); thirdly, Conservative policy was to open higher education to 'market forces'.

Consequently in 1982 the National Advisory Board [NAB] was set up to control expenditure in the Local Authority Higher Education sector and to make recommendations to the Secretary of State on the range of courses and on planning student numbers. In Stewart's opinion (1989) 'it created a new cohesion for public sector higher education'. (PSHE)

The voluntary colleges were still directly controlled by the DES but after discussion agreed to co-operate with NAB. So in 1985 the government formed a Voluntary Sector Consultative Committee (VSCC) with Dr David Harrison, Vice-Chancellor of Exeter University, as Chairman. This formulated policy and defended their interests, for example warding off, with the help of Bishop Leonard of London, a proposal to end Initial Teacher Education (ITE) at the College of St Mark and St John. Such a body was useful when the voluntary colleges had only 22,000 students to set against the Polytechnics' 185,000. The Anglican Colleges similarly formed a Council of Church College Principals [CCCP] in yet another attempt to get the surviving colleges to think confederally.

A major preoccupation for S Martin's was coping, usually at short notice, with the detailed and changing requirements of the DES and NAB as they tried to plan the numbers of teachers. One aim was to avoid over-production of secondary teachers in the late 1980s while not neglecting the 'shortage subjects' such as mathematics and physics. S Martin's was one of only two colleges given 'scholarship' places for students intending to teach these subjects but secondary PGCE targets were reduced sharply. Policy now was to insist on 'viable' groups of 12–15 in a subject so the college lost two valued courses, music and geography.

However by 1982 fears were expressed of a future shortage of primary teachers so S Martin's had its BEd and PGCE targets raised steadily.

Plans were complicated by the continued national policy of allowing new developments only if 'no extra resources were required'. So the balancing act continued since any large increase in overall totals was forbidden by NAB's rigorous procedures. Numbers in higher education were expected to fall so the BA target for 1985 was lowered from 90 to 75, and then raised to 84 for 1986 and 89 for 1987. Note the precision! Nevertheless the college's total steadily rose, exceeding 1000 (including INSET and Adult Education) by 1986 though the attempts of Charlotte Mason College to work closely with S Martin's were not followed up. Policy then changed in 1987 with the publication of the White Paper *Higher education: meeting the challenge*. This expected the age participation rate to rise from 14 per cent to 18.5 per cent with wider access from, for example, 'mature' (over 25 years old) and ethnic minority students.

Financial planning was made harder by persistent attempts by the DES to exercise tighter control with what the Bursar termed a 'fast developing centralism' through procedures which changed frequently, usually at short notice leaving little if any time for con-

sultation. As he told the Governors in February 1987, 'for the fifth successive year the format of accounts is changed. Further changes will be necessary for 1987–8'.

The Bursar's task was made even worse as estimates were increased in percentage terms while the College's record of cost-effectiveness put it at a disadvantage compared with other institutions. He wryly commented in 1984: 'Though the 1985–6 funding proposals provide some welcome easement, they seem to move us from the second worst funded voluntary college to the least funded'. However the new 'formula-funding' approach by types of degree programme proved helpful for a while until PCFC introduced yet another system from 1990 involving 'bids'. Yet

Science teaching.

The Students' Union

Social and cultural activities are vital in a college to complement the academic side and good student-staff relationships were a priority from the start at S Martin's. Students always had their own Union and accommodation, using part of the Dining Hall originally. Their own Union Building was built as soon as was feasible with a major contribution from College private funds.

Discos and other social events were regularly organised, using the large common room. Formal balls were put on with first rate music and food for, eg, 'Freshers' and 'Those Going Down' at the end of their College career. The Social Club bar was especially valuable as a meeting place for staff as well as students, offering a wide range of refreshment - non-alcoholic as well as alcoholic. A coffee bar was of great value, too, especially for non-resident students.

A good range of clubs and societies was maintained, reflecting the changing interests of successive generations. Sports and other physical activities such as outdoor pursuits were always significant. Some societies were linked with academic subjects, eg Drama and Social Ethics. Special interest groups formed societies, eg to champion animal rights or carry out projects to help the community.

Student welfare was always a major concern of the Union and responsibilities of elected officers included looking after the interests of residents, 'black' and women students. Representation on academic committees from subject departments up to the Academic Board and Governing Body played a vital part in maintaining good relationships and developing courses. The External Affairs Officer represented the Union on the National Union of Students.

All this depended on students being willing to be involved and successive Presidents played a key role. The Governing Body demonstrated that it valued this by paying half the salary of an elected 'Sabbatical' President from 1969 and latterly of a Vice-President too.

Paul Winter continued to end the financial year only a few thousands of pounds down (or up) on estimates which steadily moved towards three million pounds.

The staff-student ratio steadily deteriorated from 1:10.6 (1983) to 1:12.7 (1988), but the quality of the College's work remained sound—even good at times—in the view of its judges. No-one was made compulsorily redundant (unlike many other institutions) and the compensation system was used intelligently to enable older staff to retire. Thus vacancies were created for new academic specialists and staff from school with the 'recent and relevant' experience essential for Professional Studies.

One of the Bursar's other triumphs was building up the 'Appeal Fund' largely through income earned, with the help of David Ash's catering department, by an excellent reputation as a conference centre. This enabled the Principal's policy of 'pump-priming' projects to continue and found the governors' share of the cost of new buildings, such as the Cross Building (with drama studio) added to the Keep in 1986, or even financed complete projects such as the popular squash courts.

Rag Week.

2. *Constraints on the ITE curriculum*

Another major constraint in the 1980s was the imposition of central control on the ITE curriculum. As Locke (1985) put it, 'the question of the practicality and usefulness of the training remain[ed], as before, in doubt.' At a journalistic level juvenile disorder and falling standards were blamed on trendy young teachers. More seriously, published surveys by HMI in 1978–9 seemed to show inadequate preparation and too wide a variety of provision in ITE.

DES Circular 3/84 (April 1984) summed up the conclusions from three important papers published in the previous fifteen months, notably *Teaching quality* (March 1983). 'It is for the Secretary of State ... to say whether the course is suitable for the professional preparation of teachers.' Approval (or accreditation) was made a separate issue from academic validation so a Council for the Accreditation of Teacher Education (CATE) was set up with Professor William Taylor as its first Chairman. It was to review all existing courses and scrutinize any proposals for new ITE courses.

'Criteria' for the approval of a course were defined. It must have local support, be 'developed and run in close working partnership' with schools and be taught by lecturers with 'recent success' as school teachers. Students should have 'substantial' school experience (at least fifteen weeks on a PGCE and twenty on a BEd course). BEd students should spend the equivalent of two years on 'subject studies', including methodology. Courses should devote a 'substantial amount of time to the study of teaching language and mathematics' (at least 100 hours on each). 'The professional studies of intending teachers should, moreover, prepare them for their wider role of class teachers.'

Meeting this requirement proved increasingly difficult as the range of the primary curriculum continued to grow inexorably to culminate in the National Curriculum laid down by the 1988 Education Reform Act. This consisted of RE, three 'core' and six 'foundation' subjects, not to mention 'cross-curricular issues'. 'Educational and Professional Studies' were now to include a wide range of topics (known irreverently as the

CATE ragbag' since it was hard to treat them in any depth). Gone were the 1970s' courses in 'disciplines of education'. All this had to be fitted into effectively nine terms (after allowing for school experience, revision and examinations).

The staff naturally had been keeping in touch with these developments and teaching students about them. Rigorous HMI inspections had been experienced in 1980 (PGCE) and 1983–4 (all ITE). This had culminated in ten HMI spending a week in college in February 1984 and led to a generally favourable report (oddly not published until 1986).

Jim Garbett had a policy of reviewing courses quinquennially, so as early as March 1982 the new 1980 BEd was being appraised. Typically a staff consensus was sought, taking into account students' views too as consumers, and over the years the degree scheme was steadily modified as much as was necessary to meet the criteria.

There was no need for radical change. The College had always taken subject studies seriously (when some places had moved over to 'Applied Education'), attempted to cover the whole primary curriculum in its professional studies, and given substantial school experience. The major innovation was the reduction of Theory of Education in year 4 and the introduction of a course in the 'application of the main subject' to the learning of the primary pupil. This included placement in school and prepared the student to be a subject co-ordinator. Ironically this was greatly helped by the presence on the staff for two years of an expert in the field, Charles Desforges, who had earlier been a severe university assessor for Professional Studies. French was dropped as a main subject as primary French had gone out of fashion. The existing policy of seconding staff to teach in schools for 'professional updating' (known in College as PUD), however, now became an obligation on relevant staff. Less time was available for higher degrees.

Eventually, a revised BEd (Mark 4) was validated by the University and approved by

CATE for a 1988 start. Courses common to BEd and BA in the first and final years were retained. Important developments included widening the Early Years age-range to 3½ to 8 as more children were starting school earlier, and finding more time for the second teaching subject, science (now a 'core' subject in the National Curriculum) and technology whose importance was being stressed.

The PGCE primary course had similarly developed to meet the criteria and a demanding Nursery/Infant PGCE course started in 1989. In the 1980s the proportion of new primary teachers trained nationally by the PGCE route rose to one half. But the criteria had resulted in heavy demands on primary students, especially PGCE (even with the 36-week year), and did not leave them the proper time for reading and reflection.

3. *New course developments*

In spite of the constraints the BA courses widened with extra minor subjects and Honours programmes in geography and history. In the latter students could choose a University special subject and results compared very well with those of University students. The Ordinary BA degree died out by 1988.

However a new Ordinary degree was introduced in Community and Youth Studies. The Department's reputation had grown, in-service training for youth workers in the region had developed in partnership with the LEAs, and national policy over the provision of youth workers was also changing.

'Special initiatives' (two year PGCE courses) were launched nationally as another attempt to provide more teachers for shortage subjects. S Martin's was allowed to start 'SI' courses in mathematics and physics from 1987. These brought in interesting staff on secondment from schools as lecturers.

A Nursing degree also progressed, if slowly, towards a 1989 start. Careful negotiations with the University, local Schools of Nursing and the English Nursing Board led

American experience.

to a four-year concurrent scheme which could produce the graduate nurses with the requisite skills in one of three specialties envisaged by Project 2000. One distinctive element was the emphasis on ethical issues in nursing, drawing on the strength in social ethics.

In-service work continued to recruit over 150 fte students a year, and, as McNamara and Ross (1982, p. 79) comment, 'it provide[d] a service to practising teachers but it also ensure[d] that the initial BEd programme [was] kept in touch with developments in the schools'. Tony James had to cope with successive changes in financial and administrative arrangements as the government, dissatisfied with LEA handling of INSET, used specific grants, not just from the DES but from such agencies as the Manpower Services Commission, to direct INSET to 'priority areas'. A wide-ranging programme had been built up, including Diplomas. Tutors had to devise courses on or off site to meet a shifting market throughout Lancashire and Cumbria. A team of colleagues joined a consortium of teachers in Lancashire Polytechnic and the College of Adult Education in Chorley to provide a CNAA-validated Diploma in Educational Technology which involved the production of high quality distance-learning packages. Other notable examples were primary science in Cumbria, personal and social development of secondary pupils, and unique work with police on liaison with schools.

4. 'Enterprise S Martin's'

These last two arose from the Moral Education centre which continued its work throughout the 1980s under Mike Cross who also became editor in 1986 of a new journal entitled *Values*.

Andy Smith, under the auspices of the Health Education Council, gained a national reputation for 'Active Tutorial Work' as a method of developing personal and social skills in schools and even with long-term prisoners. This Project, like several others, involved the secondment of teachers full- or part-time to strengthen College resources.

The Institute for Educational Computing responded to demands for courses and help in curriculum development. Primed by a grant from the Department of Trade and Industry it also extended the expertise in Information Technology of College students (BA as well as BEd).

Four Vice-Principals

Three very different women and a man have served S Martin's as Vice-Principals.

DR GWEN OWEN had fought her way up the education system to achieve a PhD and become headmistress of Brighouse Girls' Grammar School. A very different character from Dr Pollard she was a useful complement to his qualities. She always made light of administration but was actually sharp and efficient. She formed a good partnership with the Dean, being in practice Dean of Women Students. Her gifts led to her becoming Principal of St Mary's College, Cheltenham, but unhappily her career ended prematurely with the cuts of the 1970s.

MARGARET WALLIS had made a sharp change of career from classics teaching to lecturing in primary education at Coventry College. A woman of deep Christian faith she showed great pastoral concern for students in trouble. She also proved a valuable foil to her Principal, Robert Clayton, who spent a lot of time off-site fighting the battles of the 1980s. She involved herself in the life of the City, notably through Save the Children Fund, and saw her mother receive Royal congratulations on her hundredth birthday.

JANET TROTTER was a formidable woman. After training as an infant teacher, she took three degrees and became Head of Professional Studies at 'King Alf's' (ie King Alfred's College, Winchester). For a time she was Assistant Secretary of the Church Colleges, which made her better known in the Church. She quickly won the respect of all at S Martin's. It was a severe blow when, after only five terms, she was called to be Principal of the combined Cheltenham colleges, St Paul and St Mary. She soon led them to amalgamate with the local College of Technology to form the Cheltenham and Gloucester College of Higher Education. Having inexhaustible energy she regularly inspected theological colleges and produced an official report on technology in education, being awarded an OBE at an unusually early age for a college principal.

JOHN CREWDSON came from Trinity and All Saints College, Leeds, with wide experience in developing courses. This proved very useful as S Martin's negotiated with schools of nursing, professional validating bodies and the University to introduce new degrees in Nursing and Health Studies. When PCFC introduced new funding arrangements, he became responsible for pricing the 'bids' for degree courses to be made by the college. As light relief, three choirs benefited from his fine bass voice.

The Institute of European Education continued its good progress under its founder, David Peacock, who left in 1985 to become Principal of Whitelands College in the Roehampton Institute of Higher Education. Attracting funds from the DES and EEC, its pioneering work on graded tests in five languages, with associated teaching packs, provided over 85,000 tests in 1983–4, and led to the formation of a special Unit to market such materials.

Debate over the curriculum for the 14 to 19 age group at a time of serious unemployment brought to the College in 1983 a '14–19 Curriculum Development Unit'. It monitored rapidly moving developments in several LEAs in response to government curriculum initiatives from not the DES but the Department of Employment via the Manpower Services Commission (MSC). These made significant sums of money available for schools and colleges when the DES was cutting back. A Youth Training Scheme had been set up for those out of work. Then MSC paid for pilot curriculum development schemes under the Technical and Vocational Education Initiative (TVEI). The Unit published a series of informative papers and then moved on to work with LEAs in evaluating such schemes.

RE in Church Schools in a multi-cultural society was the focus of the CREATE Project funded by the trust resulting from the closure of the Church College of All Saints, Tottenham. Over five years this surveyed and disseminated good RE practice in schools and aimed to promote strategies, skills and processes for teachers to manage difference and change constructively.

Some teaching materials produced by College staff achieved a wider—even national—reputation. John Holding (Head of Mathematics) had been involved in the Schools Mathematics Project (SMP) since its origin. Roy Edwards was responsible for materials in primary mathematics (such as IMP—Infant Mathematics Project) and science. Brian Gates served as Chairman of the interfaith

Religious Education Council for several years. Lois Louden, David Urwin and John Holland continued their work with the Diocese of Blackburn and other dioceses in training Aided School Governors. This became all the more important as governors were given greater responsibilities under successive Education Acts and they produced editions of an authoritative Handbook.

5. College characters and ethos

One major asset in coping with the 1980s was the continued basic stability of the staff. Consequently change was evolutionary rather than revolutionary. But an indication of the strains was the death of Harry Vickers (Head of Science) from a heart attack on his fiftieth birthday. Other Heads of Subject/Area followed Ben Holgate into early retirement.

Margaret Wallis continued her devoted work as 'Home Secretary' while Robert Clayton fought the College's battles on or off site and, with the help of his wife, Rose, strove to develop relationships with people of significance to the College. When Miss Wallis retired, greatly loved, at the end of 1984, the College was fortunate in her successor, Janet Trotter. It was remarkable how quickly she gained the respect and affection of all sections of the College community. Bringing new insights she tidied up the academic organisation so that all four Deans became, in effect, Directors of Programmes. Unfortunately, Cheltenham, being unable to find a Principal after advertisement, offered the post to Janet and she moved after only five terms. She was succeeded in September 1986 by John Crewdson from Trinity and All Saints College, Leeds.

A very dynamic Chaplain arrived at the same time, Graham Pollitt. An evangelical with an irrepressible sense of humour, he exercised a valuable pastoral ministry throughout the College community (including the rugby club). Starting a lively music group he made a great impact on college

Oratorio.

worship. He was ecumenical and a feature of chapel life was the increased involvement of Catholic students, who were now coming to S Martin's in significant numbers. In a positive report to the Governors after his first year he paid tribute to the students' commitment and effort. These were shown not only in caring effectively for each other but in such external areas as One World Week and Amnesty International. After his four year term of office he moved to be Chaplain at Cheltenham.

Led by a series of hard-working Sabbatical Presidents (like John Pearce and Ann-Marie Houghton) and Secretaries, supported by a Student Representative Council, a wide-ranging programme of student activities—social, cultural and athletic—continued. Some achieved regional or national reputation in rugby, hockey or outdoor pursuits. Charitable work continued, including helping local youth organisations and fundraising, notably through the SCAN Review. This originated as a response to Trevor Jackson who fought against leukaemia to take his degree and achieve his first promotion but died soon after in 1983. The first of what became an entertaining series of annual reviews was put on which raised valuable sums for 'Student Cancer Appeal Nationwide' (SCAN) and other good causes and helped to develop a 'Christmas spirit' at the end of term.

In 1987, John Harding secured the last 'Crombie' redundancy. Bishop Stewart Cross, chairman of Governors since 1982, retired through ill health and died in the following year. His genuine interest and concern had been deeply appreciated. Harry Harrison also had to retire. As Engineer he had carefully watched over the College's buildings and taken a thoughtful interest in its life. Andy Smith felt able to become an independent consultant and was succeeded as Head of CYS by Rev Dr Neil Kendra who also served on the relevant PCFC Programme committee.

Staff joining the College over this period placed less importance on religious aspects of the ethos established in the early days, and were not helped by any programme of staff development; the Christian influence of residential tutors declined and even some long-serving staff lost some of the early inspiration under the pressures. This was illustrated by a research project into the Church colleges.

Concern about their role and distinctive-ness had provoked further writing in the 1970s. When Culham College was closed, Revd Dr John Gay became director of the Culham College Institute for Church Related Education. He later led a carefully researched project taking as a central question: 'What justifications can be validly put forward for the retention of the Anglican colleges in the 1980s and beyond?' Lois Louden was secretary of the Church Colleges Joint Research Group which provided support to his project and discussed research issues of common concern to the colleges.

The final report after a useful series of interim papers (Gay, 1986 & 1988) showed that many outside the colleges expected them to be recognisably Christian institutions, pre-eminently concerned with training teachers, having an important role in RE and relating Christian insights to their curriculum; they felt the colleges were doing a good job. But the research also showed that college staffs—although 73 per cent claimed to have some sort of Christian affiliation—generally put more emphasis on academic and professional than religious goals. This problem—identified in 1966 by the Bishop of Salisbury's Commission (see Chapter 3)—still remained. Gay argued that attention must be paid to this deficiency or the colleges might well not be fulfilling the expected role and would lose their distinctiveness.

Although about a third of the staff actively supported local churches, the percentage of those attending chapel declined and only a few took the trouble to raise values or Christian issues explicitly. One notable exception was the Head of Educational Studies, David Urwin, who ensured that all BEd and some PGCE students were made to think about value issues in education. This supported the view of the Board of Education that a Christian Head of Education would be a crucial figure in maintaining the Church-relatedness of a College.

9

Silver Jubilee Year (1988–9)

1. *The year begins*

The twenty-fifth intake was the largest so far, with over 450 new students: Initial Teacher Education (ITE) figures were approaching the heights of the early 1970s, the Community and Youth Studies (CYS) BA recruited 26; BEd (Mark 4) was introduced at last along with a new postgraduate Diploma in CYS. Entry qualifications continued to rise (and more students came through 'Access' courses). But following national trends, ethnic minorities provided few students and the BEd intake remained predominantly female. As McNamara and Ross (1982, p. 73) commented on the BEd, 'a substantial proportion of well qualified students choose to study at a college of education, rather than at a university, because they prefer what they see as a smaller, more supportive institution which is

Jubilee Eucharist: from left to right, the Archbishop of York, Robert Clayton and Bishop Chesters.
(Lancaster Guardian)

distinctly orientated towards their future careers'. The college now had over 1200 fte students and the staff-student ratio deteriorated further to 1:13.2. The budget approached £4m.

More accommodation was being built for opening in 1989. Mr Rothen did his last designs before the Charles Pike Partnership dissolved, converting the officers' stables into two History rooms and developing a Craft, Design and Technology workshop for the Art and Design Department. To provide more student rooms—while contributing to the City's policy of revitalising old buildings—a hall of residence for 92 was converted by the canal, christened appropriately The Mill.

2. Yet another funding system: PCFC

But a main preoccupation was the introduction of yet another system of planning and funding higher education. After the 1987 White Paper, *Meeting the challenge*, the 1988 Education Reform Act set up the Polytechnics and Colleges Funding Council (PCFC) to replace the National Advisory Board for Local Authority Higher Education (NAB). Legally incorporated from November 1988 to replace NAB from 1 April 1989 ('Vesting Day'), this marked a further stage towards the eventual unification of policy making and funding arrangements for higher education as the 'binary line' set up after 1966 between universities and the 'public sector' (ie polytechnics and colleges) was steadily removed by the Conservative government.

Student numbers were to increase to an age participation rate of 18.5 per cent by 2000, but typically no commitment was made on resources to match. Higher education was to serve the economy more effectively. 'Market forces' and 'value for money' were current slogans. 'Formula funding' (under which an institution received a specific fee for a student on a specific course programme) was replaced by asking institutions to 'bid' for courses,

naming a price at which places on a particular degree 'programme' would be available. Quality and demand would influence PCFC to award a 'contract' to teach a course, but clearly relative cheapness would be another factor. Detailed bargaining over student numbers continued. Funding for in-service courses changed again too, some being 'Grant related' as the government again sought to encourage courses towards certain areas by use of specific grants.

Polytechnics were freed from any LEA control as part of the Conservative policy of reducing LEA power. Voluntary colleges thus lost a characteristic which had long made them distinctive—an independent relationship with the DES. Since the term 'voluntary college' now had little use, the Association of Voluntary Colleges was replaced by the Council of Church and Associated Colleges (CCAC) to include such colleges as Froebel and Homerton. These colleges were for the first time formally represented within the government's planning and financial structures when PCFC set up a Committee for the Church and Associated Colleges.

PCFC imposed other changes too. One was a new Instrument and Articles of Government. This would again reduce the size of S Martin's Governing Body and Academic Board. A new pay bargaining system, dominated by certain Directors of Polytechnics, was another change as each institution was now an independent employer. Its confrontational style over determining pay and conditions of service was 'most disturbing' to the Bursar and proved to be counter-productive. To facilitate staff changes a new Premature Retirement with Compensation (PRC) scheme was introduced, utilised by two college lecturers in the first year.

All this prompted a series of papers from the Principal to heads of subject, passing on unending advice from PCFC to guide planning. One interesting task imposed was the composition of a 'Mission Statement' setting out the institution's aims as an introduction to a 'Strategic Plan' for 1989–92 with a longer-term review. This posed a new version of an old problem for the Anglican colleges: how 'religious' should their mission statements be? In the judgement of Gordon McGregor, Principal of the College of Ripon and York St John (echoing his predecessor John Barnett in 1981) the colleges were generally too reluctant to declare their Christian principles. Bill Stubbs, Chief Executive of PCFC, when reviewing these plans later at a Church Colleges Conference at S Martin's, commented that the plans rarely reflected mission statements in any distinctive way.

3. *Robert Clayton to retire*

In October 1988 Robert Clayton had informed the Governing Body of his intention to retire at the end of the academic year. Don Waddell was (again) Acting Chairman since the new Instrument of Government still had not yet been officially confirmed so Bishop Alan Chesters (of Blackburn) did not become Chairman until later in 1989. A small group of five governors was set up which appointed Dr Dorian Edynbry to be Principal. He was Vice-Principal of Worcester College of Higher Education and had previous Polytechnic experience.

4. *Silver Jubilee Celebrations*

Celebrating the College's Silver Jubilee made Mr Clayton's final year more enjoyable with its varied programme of events. He had worked hard to encourage the Old Students'

Degree Day, 1986.

Association and appropriately former students held two reunions; staff held a reunion too. Music students returned to provide soloists for Vaughan Williams' *Serenade to music*, Gillian Weir tested the Collins organ almost beyond its limits in a splendid recital, The Academy of St Martin-in-the-Fields, directed by Iona Brown, and the Haffner Orchestra gave concerts. There were varied dramatic events, including, of course, a Jubilee SCAN Review at Christmas. Professional events included a Science Funday, an Early Years conference and a Mathematics Open Day.

Since 1989 also marked 150 years of Church colleges, a group attended the service in Westminster Abbey, addressed by the Archbishop of Canterbury, Dr Runcie. College religious events included a eucharist on S Martin's Day celebrated by the first chaplain, Nigel Kinsella, a Hot Gospel concert and a commemorative service in June. This was graced by the Visitor, the Archbishop of York, Dr John Habgood. He gave a typically thoughtful sermon and planted a tree when opening a wildlife garden behind the dining room.

The University paid a nice tribute when, at the College's degree ceremony at Bailrigg, the Chancellor, HRH Princess Alexandra, also conferred the degree of LLD on Don Waddell and Hugh Pollard.

5. S Martin's at Robert Clayton's departure

What sort of college did Robert Clayton leave on his retirement? The first section of the Strategic Plan gives his official account derived from the mission statement:

Honorary degrees for Hugh Pollard and Don Waddell. From left to right: Professor Hanham; Dr Pollard; Princess Alexandra; Don Waddell. (Lancaster Guardian)

The College's religious context and commitment is demonstrated by the kind of caring community developed; by the nature of the curricula and research developments; by the close and active relationships with the Anglican Dioceses and with those of other Christian denominations and other faiths.

The College welcomes those of other denominations, of other faiths or of none, and seeks to nurture appropriate discussion of moral, ethical, social, political, religious and philosophical issues. From the outset the College has taken pains to be a caring institution, human in scale, and committed to the view that value questions cannot be ignored.

The Chapel and Chaplaincy are central within the College and especially so for arranging worship and fellowship. High quality residential, cultural, social and recreational provision exists, and the Students' Union plays a valued part in its administration.

An open, participatory style of College management enables a wide range of information to be available to all and for all to contribute to discussion and decision-making. The senior management team meets regularly to effect policy and decision-making of immediate concern. Within the last five years the College's management and organisation were studied by both Coopers and Lybrand and Hay MSL and highly commended by them.

The College's teaching strengths are in teacher education, Community and Youth Studies, Nursing and Health Studies and combined BA honours degrees which relate to and support many of the College's other courses, including the long established MA in Religious Education. For many years the college has been active in research and curriculum development in teacher education. This is reflected in the work of the College's Institutes, which include Educational Computing, Primary Education, Management of Learning (incorporating the 14–19s Unit) and European Education (with its Graded Languages Testing Unit). The current Religious Education Curriculum Project and the Moral Education Resource Centre emphasise other particular strengths. The BA degree in Social Ethics is unique within Britain. The long established MA in Religious Education recruits nationally and internationally. Developments in Nursing Studies and those proposed for training for ministry in the church (a BA proposed for 1990) will further consolidate the College's priorities which clearly remain largely in the field of the 'caring professions'.

The College's validating Body is the University of Lancaster. The relationship with the university is close, developing and active for both staff and students. Shared teaching has long been a feature at both undergraduate and postgraduate levels. Additionally other sharing of resources exists.

Our Urban Studies Centre in the East End of London represents a major collaboration (four church Colleges) and Church of England investment. Its two-site accommodation for teaching and residence provides a highly relevant urban priority area location for placement experience for students training for the caring professions and was commended in the Church of England report, *Faith in the City*.

Professor Ross's assessment to the National Advisory Board in 1983 had remained true. S Martin's 'displayed a commendable caution in developing a tight, closely integrated programme of courses ... There is a well-developed In-Service side which naturally draws on the teaching strengths provided by the initial training (including youth work) and which serves North Lancashire and Cumbria.'

HMI after yet another series of visits in late 1988 were complimentary about the initial teacher training, though this was not what some politicians wanted to hear. 'The quality of the professional training offered in BEd and PGCE courses is more than satisfactory, much of it is good and some elements of the work are outstanding. ... The students are generally articulate and confident in their oral responses in most subjects. ... Relationships between staff and students are excellent. ... The staff are well qualified and more than ¾ hold higher degrees. Nearly half the staff (of 85) have been in post for less than five years and bring recent and extensive primary experience to the ITT courses. ...'

Degree results continued to illustrate the college's teaching quality. Typically half obtained lower Second class degrees, all the more praiseworthy when one recollects their average entry qualifications. Thirds and Fails were rare. Occasionally a student achieved a First.

6. Conclusion

The College remained a good example of Locke's (1985) comments (quoted earlier) that some colleges of higher education 'used their historic features to advantage', for example small size, quality of life, religious basis (p. 102). 'Course approval mechanisms tended to be conservative in course development or at least to restrict innovation to cautious extensions of the college's range of work.' (p. 104) Only in the late 1980s was S Martin's able to exploit the new atmosphere and extend into Youth Work (including a special course for ethnic minority students with few academic qualifications), Nursing, radiography, and new forms of initial teacher education such as the two-year 'Licensed Teacher' scheme in East London schools.

Epilogue

In 1958 the Church of England Board of Education had confidently claimed: 'The expansion programme ... represents an investment of Church money which it would scarcely be possible to better'. (CA, 1958 b, para. 21) So in the post war period up to 1974 over £3m of central Church funds and £2.5m of college governors' funds were spent as the Church's share of the costs of expanding twenty-five teacher training colleges and founding two; the cost to public funds was over £15m. (GS Misc 194, p. 25)

Looking back after thirty years it is hard to say that this was such a good investment. But no-one could have foreseen the huge expansion in higher education since the Robbins Report of 1963. The Church of England's presence became far less significant numerically—but it continued in much more diverse ways.

In 1989 two Church colleges worked in an ecumenical federation and two had been federated with LEA institutions. The assets of others which had been closed continued as trusts, (such as All Saints, Culham, Durham and Exeter) which actively involved the Church in important research and other support for higher education (for example chaplaincies, teaching posts, student grants). Nine 'free-standing' colleges remained (two resulting from mergers of two colleges), almost all taking on additional work besides teacher education. Two of these nine were the new colleges founded in the 1960s, each alongside a new university.

But the same questions continued. In what lay the distinctiveness claimed by the Church colleges as their contribution and how could it be maintained? Catholic colleges traditionally had a clear function—to recruit Catholics to train as teachers for Catholic schools. The Church of England faced its long-standing educational dilemma—how to achieve successfully its 'twin aims' of serving the community as well as the Church. Moreover its traditional role as the 'Established Church' made it fearful of becoming merely a 'sect' and setting up 'ghettoes' in its colleges. Consequently in the expansion of the 1960s too much of the Anglican ethos was allowed to disappear.

As American Catholics had found in the 1960s, when investigating their colleges—and as Gay also proved in the 1986 Culham project—a church-related college has three types of goal: academic, professional and religious; in times of pressure it is the academic (and professional) goals which receive priority. S Martin's did not escape this tendency. But even the Bishop of Salisbury's Working Party in 1966 had declared: 'All things being equal, the preservation of academic excellence is of prime importance'. (p. 16)

In all this, staff are fundamental. McNamara and Ross (1982, p. 73) wrote: 'The essence of an educational institution is the competence and values of the people who serve it. As they say in the navy, it's not the ship that matters but the crew that's on it'. Not enough able committed Christians came forward to provide what Gordon McGregor maintained was a crucially distinctive feature of a Church college: providing 'high quality education in a context in which the practice and study of the Christian faith are taken seriously'. (Brighton, 1990, p. 174) This also was true of S Martin's as it recruited able new staff in the 1980s, though the study of beliefs

A field trip.

and values remained significant in academic and professional courses. Consequently much of the enthusiasm for maintaining an explicit Christian ethos, which was possible in the early days of a small college led by a highly committed principal, faded away. Christian values became more implicit. But the ecumenical chaplaincy continued to bear witness and, as Bishop Bulley had foreseen, its greatest success was with the teacher training students in college for four years.

Yet Canon Robertson's judgement remains a valid justification for S Martin's: 'The colleges are a tense blend of the faith community and the plural, neutral secular community. Within that tension, they offer an opportunity to witness to generations who are otherwise only marginally touched by the Church.' (GS Misc 16, 1972, para. 53)

So, under the enterprising leadership of two very different Principals, though the Christian ethos became more problematic, S Martin's retained its identity. Moreover, it emerged from a stormy period for higher education with useful potential for serving the church as it faced the next challenge—rapid expansion into a still greater diversity of courses for a wider range of students.

Hard at work in the Library.

Bibliography

Alexander R. J., Craft M. and Lynch J. (eds) (1984) *Change in teacher education: context and provision since Robbins,* Holt, Rinehart & Winston.

Board of Education (1944) *Teachers and youth leaders* (MacNair Report), HMSO.

Brighton T. (ed) (1989) *150 years: the Church colleges in higher education,* West Sussex Institute of Higher Education.

Church Assembly of the Church of England:

(1945) *The key to Christian education,* Council of Church Training Colleges.

(1949) *The development of the Church training colleges,* (CA 931).

(1957) *The capital needs of the Church training colleges,* (CA 1213).

(1958 a) *The expansion of the Church training colleges for teachers,* (CA 1266).

(1958 b) *The expansion of Church training colleges,* Central Board of Finance (CAF 278).

(1959 a) *The expansion of Church training colleges for teachers,* Board of Education (CA 1277).

(1959 b) *The expansion of Church training colleges: a further report by the Central Board of Finance,* (CAF 279).

(1961) *A report by the Board of Education,* (CA 1359).

(1962) *The expansion of the Church training colleges,* (CA 1422).

(1963) *The expansion of the Church training colleges—a progress report,* (CA 1457).

(1967) *The Church colleges of education: report of the working party on the communication of the Christian faith* (Bishop of Salisbury's Commission), (CA 1654).

Dent H. C. (1977) *The training of teachers in England and Wales, 1800–1975,* Hodder & Stoughton.

Department of Education and Science (1972) *Teacher education and training* (James Report), HMSO.

Department of Education and Science (1972) *Education: a framework for expansion,* White Paper, HMSO.

Department of Education and Science (1983) *Teaching quality,* HMSO.

Department of Education and Science (1983) *Teaching in schools: the content of initial teacher training,* HMSO.

Department of Education and Science (1987) *Higher education: meeting the challenge,* White Paper, HMSO.

Faith in the city (1985) (The report of the Archbishop of Canterbury's Commission on Urban Priority Areas), Church House Publishing.

Francis L. and Thatcher A. (eds) (1990) *Christian perspectives for education,* Gracewing.

Gay J. D. (1978) *The Christian campus? the role of the English churches in higher education,* Culham College Institute, Abingdon.

Gay J. D. (1986) *The future of the Anglican colleges* (Final report of the Church Colleges Research Project), Culham College Institute, Abingdon.

Gay J. D. (1988) 'The churches and the training of teachers in England and Wales' in McClelland V. A. (ed) *Christian education in a pluralist society,* Routledge & Kegan Paul.

Gedge P. S. (1974) *The role of a Church of England College of Education* (unpublished MEd thesis) University of Birmingham.

Gedge P. S. (1981) 'The Church of England Colleges since 1944', *Journal of Educational Administration and History,* XIII (1) 33–42.

General Synod of the Church of England, Board of Education (1974) *The future of the Church Colleges of Education,* (GS 194), Church House, London.

General Synod of the Church of England, Board

of Education (1974) *The future of the Church colleges: continuity of function in mergers and federations*, (GS Misc. 29), Church House, London.

Hencke D. (1978) *Colleges in crisis*, Penguin.

Hewett S. (ed) (1971) *The training of teachers—a factual survey*, University of London Press.

Higher education (Robbins Report) HMSO, 1963.

Locke M. *et al* (1985) *The colleges of higher education from 1972 to 1982*, Critical Press, Croydon.

McClintock M. (1974) *The University of Lancaster: quest for innovation*, The University, Lancaster.

McGregor G. P. (1981) *Bishop Otter College and policy for teacher education, 1839–1980*, Pembridge Press.

McGregor G. P. (1991) *A Church College for the 21st Century? 150 years of Ripon & York St John*, University College of Ripon and York St John.

McNamara D. and Ross A. (1982) *The BEd degree and its future*, University of Lancaster School of Education.

National Society (1943) *The Church training colleges*, Great Peter Street, London.

Niblett W. R. (1978) *The Church's Colleges of Higher Education*, Church Information Office.

Pollard H. M. (1956) *Pioneers of popular education*, Murray.

Pye M. (1977) *The language of the Church in higher and further education: an account of the Bradwell Consultation*, Church House, London.

Rose M. (1981) *A history of King Alfred's College, Winchester, 1840–1980*, Phillimore, Chichester.

Seaman R. D. H. (1978) *St Peter's College, Saltley, 1944–78*, St Peter's College.

Sharp P. R. (1987) *The creation of the local authority sector of higher education*, Falmer Press.

Stewart W. A. C. (1989) *Higher education in post war Britain*, Macmillan.

Appendices

Admissions

Year	Teachers' Cert	BEd 4th Year	BEd	PGCE sec.	PGCE prim.	BA	Total
1964	89						89
1965	175						250
1966	168			10			410
1967	193			33			525
1968	170	20		109			678
1969	203	20		137			728
1970	193	30		148			740
1971	194	30		148	38		772
1972	179	31		138	42		740
1973	175	24		132	30		763
1974	167	57		130	38		730
1975		53	133	127	43		688
1976		66	119	135	43		699
1977		51	113	123	32		676
1978			92	149	30	19	693
1979			94	139	36	19	721
1980			70	166	35	61	770
1981			78	141	32	77	746
1982			87	119	15	91	798
1983			92	86	22	92	800
1984			103	83	22	95	892
1985			129	85	27	85	945
1986			120	109	32	92	1031
1987			140	126	36	110	1120
1988			137	114	42	127	1250

Staff visit to Rose Castle, 1969.

Senior Staff
(in order of appointment)

Brackets are used to indicate degrees awarded after joining the staff and destinations.

1964 Gwen Owen, BSc, PhD. Vice-Principal (Principal of St Mary's College, Cheltenham, 1970)

Bill Etherington, MA (MEd). Head of Education and Dean of Men Students (Principal of Keswick Hall College of Education, 1973)

Colin Aiston, BSc (MA). Mathematics; later Senior Tutor. (retired, 1985)

John Jennings, MA (DPhil). Geography. (retired, 1983)

Peter Moore, MA (BPhil), FRCO. Music. (retired, 1984)

Revd Gordon Pavey, BD, MEd. Theology. (College of St Matthias, Fishponds, 1968)

Harry Vickers, BSc (MSc). Biology; later Science. (died 1985)

Frank Warren, MA (MA(Ed)). English. (retired 1983)

John Chippendale, MB, BCh. Medical Officer. (retired 1990)

Ernest Helm, DPA. Bursar. (retired 1975)

Hilda Stoddard, BA. (Chester College, 1977)

1965 Tony Cooper, MA, BLitt. History. (Avery Hill College, 1975)

Ray Halliday, BA (MA). Modern Languages. (retired 1989)

Ben Holgate, ATD (MA). Art. (retired 1981)

1966 Keith Lockett, BSc. Physics. (New Zealand, 1972)

Barry Ogden, BSc (MSc). Chemistry; later Head of PGCE and Dean. (retired 1992)

1967 John Holding, MA. Mathematics. (retired 1986)

Jim Garbett, MA (MA(Ed)) (joined staff 1967). PGCE; later Head of Educational Studies, Dean.

1968 Brenda Harding, BD. (joined staff 1965) Theology. (left 1970, later principal lecturer at Charlotte Mason College)

1970 Margaret Wallis, BA. Vice Principal. (retired 1984)

Peter Gedge, MA (MEd). (joined staff 1968) Theology; later PGCE, Professional Studies, Dean of BA Studies. (retired 1990)

1972 Kevin Lambert, BSc, MSc. Physics. (Adviser in Dudley, 1975)

1973 Cdr Gerry Tordoff, BSc. Registrar. (retired 1984)

Tony James, BSc, MEd. (joined staff 1969) Inservice; later Dean.

1975 Brian Gates, MA, STM (PhD). Religious Studies and Social Ethics.

Margaret Shennan, BA. (joined staff 1972) History. (retired 1984)

1976 Paul Winter, ABIM, (BA) Bursar.

Heads of Area were introduced:

Elizabeth Green, (MA). (joined staff 1971) Primary PGCE. (retired 1987)

John Holland, MA (MA(Ed)). (joined staff 1967) Professional Studies.

Peter Jennings, (MEd) (joined staff 1967) PE, Educational Studies Part I. (retired 1990)

Lois Louden, BSc, MA, PhD. (joined staff 1975) PGCE Education. (retired 1990)

Revd Birman Nottingham, MA, MEd, (PhD). (joined staff 1966). Advanced Professional Studies. (retired 1983)

Revd David Peacock, BA (MA). (joined staff 1967). School Experience; later Director of Institute of European Education. (Principal of Whitelands College, 1985)

David Urwin, MA (MA(Ed)). (joined staff 1966) Educational Studies. (retired 1990)

1977 Jean Stearns (Garriock), MA. Librarian. (retired 1989)

1978 Anthony Kearney, BA, MLitt. Co-ordinator, BA English Literature. (retired 1991)

1979 Margaret Whiteside, BA (MSc) (joined staff 1967) School Experience, later Director of Institute of European Education. (retired 1990)

1981 Bob Lewis, BSc, MSc. Institute of Educational

Computing. (University of Lancaster, 1985)

Andy Smith, (MEd) (joined staff 1976) Community and Youth Studies. (own consultancy, 1988)

1982 Ray Haslam, ATD, (MA) (joined staff 1972) Art.

1983 David Aitken, BA, MA. (joined staff 1965) English. (retired 1991)

Jim Price, BA (MSc). (joined staff 1970) Geography.

1984 Teresa Abramson, BA. (joined staff 1979) Registrar.

Roger Cann, MusB (MMus). (joined staff 1966) Music. (retired 1992)

Peter Knight, BA (PhD). (joined staff 1981)

History. (University of Lancaster, 1990)

1985 Janet Trotter, MA, MSc, BD. Vice Principal (Principal of College of St Paul and St Mary, Cheltenham, 1986)

Sheila Jelly, BSc, MEd. (joined staff 1983) Science. (Rolle College, 1988)

1986 Philip Gager, BSc, MSc, PhD. Mathematics. John Crewdson, MA. Vice Principal.

1987 Roy Edwards, (MEd). (joined staff 1968) Primary PGCE. (retired 1991)

1988 Revd Neil Kendra, BA, MSc, PhD. Community and Youth Studies. Alf Anderson, BSc, MSc. Science.

1989 David Brown, BA. Librarian.

Abbreviations

BA	Bachelor of Arts degree	ITE	Initial Teacher Education
BEd	Bachelor of Education degree	ITT	Initial Teacher Training
CATE	Council for the Accreditation of Teacher Education	LEA	Local Education Authority
CNAA	Council for National Academic Awards	NAB	National Advisory Board for Higher Education
CYS	Community and Youth Studies (a College course)	PCFC	Polytechnics and Colleges Funding Council
DASE	Diploma in the Advanced Study of Education	PGCE	Post Graduate Certificate in Education (qualification)
DES	Department of Education and Science	PSHE	Public sector higher education (as distinct from universities)
FTE	Full time equivalent (students)		
GCE	General Certificate of Education	RAC	Regional Advisory Council for Further Education
GCSE	General Certificate of Secondary Education		
HMI	Her Majesty's Inspector(s) of Schools	VSCC	Voluntary Sector Consultative Council (of Church colleges)
INSET	In-Service Education and Training (for teachers)		

Occasional Papers from the Centre for North-West Regional Studies

Flowering Plants and Ferns of Cumbria	G. Halliday	£2.95
Early Lancaster Friends	M. Mullet	£2.95
North-West Theses and Dissertations, 1950–78	U. Lawler	£6.00
Lancaster: The Evolution of its Townscape to 1800	S. Penney	£2.95
Richard Marsden and the Preston Chartists, 1837–48	J. King	£2.95
The Grand Theatre, Lancaster	A. Betjemann	£2.95
Popular Leisure and the Music Hall in 19th-century Bolton	R. Poole	£2.95
The Diary of William Fisher of Barrow, 1811–59	W. Rollinson/B. Harrison	£2.95
Rural Life in South-West Lancashire, 1840–1914	A. Mutch	£3.95
Grand Fashionable Nights: Kendal Theatre, 1575–1985	M. Eddershaw	£3.95
The Roman Fort and Town of Lancaster	D. Shotter/A. White	£4.95
Windermere in the nineteenth century	O. M. Westall	£4.95
A Traditional Grocer: T. D. Smith's of Lancaster	M. Winstanley	£4.95
Reginald Farrer: Dalesman, Planthunter, Gardener	J. Illingworth/J. Routh	£4.95
Walking Roman Roads in Bowland	P. Graystone	£4.95
The Royal Albert: Chronicles of an Era	J. Alston	£4.95
From Lancaster to the Lakes – The Region in Literature	K. Hanley/A. Milbank	£5.95
The Buildings of Georgian Lancaster	A. White	£5.95
Lydia Becker and The Cause	A. Kelly	£5.95
Romans and Britons in North-West England	D. Shotter	£5.95

Each of these titles may be ordered by post from:

C.N.W.R.S.,
Fylde College,
University of Lancaster,
Bailrigg, Lancaster

Books will be despatched post free to UK addresses.
Please make cheques payable to 'The University of Lancaster'.
Titles are also available from all good booksellers within the region.